TOP **10**
BOSTON

Top 10 Boston Highlights

The Top 10 of Everything

CONTENTS

Boston Area by Area

Streetsmart

Within each Top 10 list in this book, no hierarchy of quality or popularity is implied. All 10 are, in the editor's opinion, of roughly equal merit.
    Throughout this book, floors are referred to in accordance with American usage: i.e., the "first floor" is at ground level.

***Title page, front cover and spine** The historic Old State House on Washington Street*
***Back cover, clockwise from top left** Boston Public Library; Boston Common in winter; Downtown Boston; Old State House; Public Garden*

The rapid rate at which the world is changing is constantly keeping the DK Eyewitness team on our toes. While we've worked hard to ensure that this edition of Boston is accurate and up-to-date, we know that opening hours alter, standards shift, prices fluctuate, places close and new ones pop up in their stead. So, if you notice we've got something wrong or left something out, we want to hear about it. Please get in touch at **travelguides@dk.com**

Welcome to
Boston

City of the future, cradle of American history. Hotbed of innovation, bastion of tradition. The cultural and intellectual hub of New England, Boston is the gateway to the region with its wealth of attractions concentrated in this singular, compact city. It dazzles with renowned museums, great shopping, and lush gardens and parks. With DK Eyewitness Top 10 Boston, it's yours to explore.

The fastest way to fall in love with Boston is to explore it on foot. Walk the **Freedom Trail** through the heart of Downtown and North End to famous Revolutionary War sites, including the **Paul Revere House**, **Old North Church**, and **Faneuil Hall**. You can then explore the vibrant beauty of **Boston Common and Public Garden**, the majesty of **Trinity Church**, and the fun of high-fashion shopping along **Newbury Street**.

When you are ready for a taste of culture, what could be better than an evening listening to the fabled **Boston Symphony Orchestra**, or a visit to the **Museum of Fine Arts, Boston**, or the delightfully eccentric **Isabella Stewart Gardner Museum**? And be sure to explore the remarkable science and art museums of **Harvard University**.

Did we mention the food? With the Atlantic Ocean as its front door and the farms of New England close by, it's no wonder that Boston is renowned for great seafood and farm-to-table fare, not to mention a wealth of delicious dishes from every part of the world.

Whether you're visiting for a weekend or a week, our Top 10 guide brings together the best of everything the city has to offer, from the historic **Beacon Hill** to the lively **Theater District**. The guide has useful tips throughout, from seeking out what's free to places off the beaten path, plus 10 easy-to-follow itineraries, designed to tie together a clutch of sights in a short space of time. Add inspiring photography and detailed maps, and you've got the essential pocket-sized travel companion. **Enjoy the book, and enjoy Boston**.

Clockwise from top: **Financial District as seen from Boston Harbor, Federal-style rowhouses in Beacon Hill, Boston's Museum of Fine Arts, a brass marker on the Freedom Trail, Boston Common in fall, buoys in Rockport, Harvard University's Memorial Hall**

Exploring Boston

Whether you have just a couple of days, or more time to explore, there's so much to see and do in Boston. Here are some ideas for how to make the most of your time.

Public Garden is a vibrant green space in the heart of the city.

Two Days in Boston

Key
━ Two-day itinerary
┅ Four-day itinerary

Day ❶

MORNING

Begin at **Boston Common and Public Garden** (see pp18–19), and pick up a map for the **Freedom Trail** (see pp12–15) at the information kiosk. Walk the trail, stopping at **Faneuil Hall** (see p13) for lunch and to shop for souvenirs.

AFTERNOON

Continue along the Freedom Trail to the **Charlestown Navy Yard** (see pp36–7), and then explore the **Museum of Science** (see pp16–17). Pay a visit to **Harvard University** (see pp20–23) for a leisurely walk around campus and then take in a concert at **Sanders Theatre** (see p55).

Day ❷

MORNING

Start off at the **Museum of Fine Arts, Boston** (see pp28–31) and then see the exquisite collections of the **Isabella Stewart Gardner Museum** (see pp34–5). Have lunch at **Café G** (see p121).

AFTERNOON

Discover the Romanesque Revival beauty of **Trinity Church** (see pp32–3) before exploring **Newbury Street** (see pp24–5) shops. In the evening, enjoy a show at the **Boch Center – Wang Theatre** (see p54).

Four Days in Boston

Day ❶

MORNING

From **Boston Common and Public Garden** (see pp18–19) explore **Beacon Hill** (see pp80–85) and the antiques shops of **Charles Street** (see p69). Stop for lunch at **Artù** (see p85).

AFTERNOON

Visit the **Isabella Stewart Gardner Museum** (see pp34–5) then dine at **Sorellina** (see p93) before a performance at **Symphony Hall** (see p54).

Day ❷

MORNING

Explore **Back Bay** (see pp86–93) by visiting **Trinity Church** (see pp32–3), the **Boston Public Library** (see p87),

Boston waterfront has several attractions, including the Boston Tea Party Ships and Museum.

Trinity Church is famed for its beautiful stained glass.

and the art galleries and shops that make **Newbury Street** (see p91) a shopper's paradise.

AFTERNOON
Spend the afternoon at the **Museum of Fine Arts, Boston** (see pp28–31), followed by a waterside seafood dinner at **Legal Harborside** (see p64).

Day ❸
MORNING
Walk the **Freedom Trail** (see pp12–15), pausing at **Faneuil Hall** (see p13) for coffee and a snack. At the end of the trail, tour the **Charlestown Navy Yard** (see pp36–7) and stop for lunch at the historic **Warren Tavern** (see p37).

AFTERNOON
Head over to the **New England Aquarium** (see pp38–9) and marvel at the marine life on display. Then take in the nearby **Boston Tea Party Ships**

and Museum (see p96), joining in with the revolutionary fun. Complete the day with **Boston Harbor Cruises** (see p139), on a boat departing from **Long Wharf** (see p46).

Day ❹
MORNING
Start at the **John F. Kennedy Library and Museum** (see p133) before exploring the campus at JFK's alma mater, **Harvard University** (see pp20–23).

AFTERNOON
After lunch in **Harvard Square** (see p70) and a browse around its bookstores (see p69), visit the **Harvard Museums of Science and Culture** (see p123) and then head over to the family-friendly **Museum of Science** (see pp16–17). If the Red Sox are playing an evening game, head over to **Fenway Park** (see p117), but if you can't get hold of tickets, just make your way to **Game On!** (see p120), the on-site sports bar, and watch a live broadcast there.

Top 10 Boston Highlights

Courtyard of the Isabella Stewart Gardner Museum

🔟 Boston Highlights

With its colonial-era architecture, lively seafaring heritage, and irrepressible Yankee character, Boston is one of the country's most distinctive locales. And, for all its big-city amenities – world-class restaurants, museums, and stores – visitors find it delightfully compact and walkable.

The Freedom Trail ①
Boston's best walking tour is free, full of history, and open year round. It passes various sights, including the Paul Revere House where items such as colonial banknotes can be seen *(see pp12–15)*.

Museum of Science ②
One of Boston's liveliest and most-visited science museums, this remarkable facility delights with over 700 fascinating interactive exhibits *(see pp16–17)*.

Boston Common and Public Garden ③
In the Public Garden, swan boats drift beneath weeping willows, while on Boston Common, children splash in the Frog Pond. Don't miss the moving Shaw Memorial *(see pp18–19)*.

Harvard University ④
Established in 1636, the undisputed heart of American academia has cultivated some of the world's greatest thinkers and statespersons, including eight US presidents *(see pp20–23)*.

5 Around Newbury Street
Nowhere are the city's myriad fashions, faces, and fortunes on more vibrant display than Newbury Street, where fashionistas share the sidewalk with punk rockers *(see pp24–5)*.

6 Museum of Fine Arts, Boston
Boston's largest art museum has one of the most extensive collections of Japanese, ancient Egyptian, and Impressionist works of art in the Americas *(see pp28–31)*.

0 meters	600
0 yards	600

7 Trinity Church
This Romanesque Revival church is considered the finest work by architect H. H. Richardson. Equally impressive is La Farge's *Christ in Majesty* window *(see pp32–3)*.

8 Isabella Stewart Gardner Museum
Masterpieces by the likes of Rembrandt, Botticelli, and Raphael look magnificent in Isabella Stewart Gardner's Venetian-style palazzo, which is built around a leafy court-yard *(see pp34–5)*.

9 Charlestown Navy Yard
Boston's deep harbor was ideal for one of the US Navy's first shipyards. The USS *Constitution*, built in 1797 (3 years prior to the Yard), is still docked here *(see pp36–7)*.

10 New England Aquarium
Get to know about two species of penguins, playful harbor seals, and other creatures of the deep here *(see pp38–9)*.

TOP 10 ⭐ The Freedom Trail

Snaking through 2.5 miles (4 km) of city streets, the Freedom Trail is a living link to Boston's key revolutionary and colonial-era sites. As you walk it, you'll feel like you're treading a timeline between the past and the present. Some of Boston's most cosmopolitan stores, restaurants, and attractions are also located along the Trail.

1 Massachusetts State House

Boston architect Charles Bulfinch's *pièce de résistance*, the "new" State House (completed in 1798) is one of the city's most distinctive buildings *(see p81)*.

6 Old State House

Built in 1713, this colonial building **(left)** was the headquarters of the colonial legislature and the Royal Governor. The Declaration of Independence was first read from the balcony of this house *(see p101)*.

4 King's Chapel

The current granite building *(see p103)* dates from around 1749, but the chapel was originally founded in 1686 by King James II as an outpost of the Anglican Church. Don't miss the burying ground next door, which shelters Massachusetts' first Governor, John Winthrop *(see p44)*.

2 Park Street Church

Founded by a small group of Christians disenchanted with their Unitarian-leaning congregation, Park Street Church **(above)** was dedicated in 1810.

5 Old South Meeting House

Since the colonial era, Boston's Old South Meeting House *(see p102)* has been a crucible in the fight against slavery and for free speech.

3 Old Granary Burying Ground

A veritable who's-who of revolutionary history fertilizes this plot **(right)** next to Park Street Church. One of the most venerable residents here *(see p101)* is Samuel Adams *(see p44)*.

7 Faneuil Hall and Quincy Market

Known as the "Cradle of Liberty," Faneuil Hall *(see p101)* has played host to many revolutionary meetings in its time. Neighboring Quincy Market **(below)**, built in the early 1800s, once housed the city's wholesale food distribution.

AN HOUR OF FREEDOM

For visitors tight on time, consider this condensed trail. Head up Tremont Street from Park Street "T" station, stopping to visit the Old Granary Burying Ground. At the corner of Tremont and School streets – site of King's Chapel – turn right onto School and continue to Washington Street and the Old South Meeting House. Turn left on Washington to the Old State House then finish up at Faneuil Hall nearby on Congress Street.

8 Paul Revere House

In North Square, Paul Revere House *(see p95)* is Boston's oldest private residence. Its namesake *(see p44)* was well-regarded locally as a metalsmith prior to his history-changing ride.

10 Old North Church

This church **(below)** has a pivotal place in revolutionary history *(see p95)*. Prior to his midnight ride, Revere *(see p44)* ordered Robert Newman to hang one or two lamps in the belfry to indicate, respectively, whether the British were approaching by land or via the Charles River.

NEED TO KNOW

MAP P4 ■ Start point: Boston Common. "T" station: Park St (red/green lines) ■ Finish point: Charlestown "T" station: Community College (orange line) ■ www.thefreedomtrail.org

Park Street Church: 1 Park St; 617 523 3383; www.parkstreet.org

■ Indulge your sweet tooth at Mike's Pastry *(see p98)*.

■ Maps of the Trail are available at the Boston Common Visitor Center, or at the Boston National Park headquarters at Faneuil Hall, where free, ranger-led walking tours are offered by the National Park Service.

■ Most of the Trail is indicated in red paint with a few sections in red brick.

9 Copp's Hill Burying Ground

With headstones dating from the 17th century, Copp's Hill *(see p95)* is a must for history buffs. It was named after William Copp, a farmer who sold the land to the church.

Moments in Revolutionary History

A scene depicting American and British troops during the Battle of Lexington

1 Resistance to the Stamp Act (1765)

The king imposed a stamp duty on all published materials in the colonies, including newspapers. Furious Bostonians boycotted British goods in response.

2 Boston Massacre (1770)

Angry colonists picked a fight with British troops in front of the Old State House (see p12), resulting in the deaths of five unarmed Bostonians.

3 Samuel Adams' Tea Tax Speech (1773)

Adams' incendiary speech during a forum at the Old South Meeting House inspired the Boston Tea Party, the most subversive action undertaken yet in the debate over colonial secession.

4 Boston Tea Party (1773)

Led by Samuel Adams, the Sons of Liberty boarded three British East India Company ships and dumped their cargo into the Boston Harbor, a watershed moment of colonial defiance.

5 Paul Revere's Ride (1775)

Revere rode to Lexington to warn revolutionaries Samuel Adams and John Hancock that British troops intended to arrest them. One of the bravest acts of the war, it would be immortalized in the Longfellow poem *The Midnight Ride of Paul Revere*.

6 Battle of Lexington (1775)

Revere's ride was followed by the first exchange of fire between the ragtag colonist army and the British at Lexington.

7 Battle of Bunker Hill (1775)

The colonists' fortification of Charlestown resulted in a full-scale British attack. Despite their defeat, the colonists' resolve was galvanized by this battle.

8 Washington Takes Command (1776)

The Virginia plantation owner George Washington led the newly formed Continental Army south from Cambridge to face British troops in New Jersey.

Bust of George Washington, Old North Church

9 Fortification of Dorchester Heights (1776)

Fortifying the mouth of Boston Harbor with a captured cannon, George Washington put the Royal Navy under his guns and forced a British retreat from the city.

10 Declaration of Independence (1776)

On July 4, the colonies rejected all allegiance to the British Crown. In Boston, independence was declared from the Royal Governor's head-quarters, the building known today as the Old State House (see p12).

MASSACHUSETTS STATE HOUSE

Finished in 1798, the State House is Charles Bulfinch's masterwork. With its brash design details, imposing stature, and liberal use of fine materials, it embodies the optimism of post-revolutionary America. The building is in three distinct sections: the original Bulfinch front; the marble wings constructed in 1917; and the yellow-brick 1895 addition, known as the Brigham Extension after the architect who designed it. Just below Bulfinch's central colonnade, statues of famous Massachusetts figures strike poses. Among them are the great orator Daniel Webster; President John F. Kennedy; and Quaker Mary Dyer, who was hanged in 1660 for challenging the authority of Boston's religious leaders. Directly below the State House's immense gilded dome is the Senate Chamber, site of many influential speeches and debates. After an extensive renovation, the historic chamber reopened in early 2019.

TOP 10
STATE HOUSE FEATURES

1 23-carat gold dome

2 Senate Chamber

3 House of Representatives

4 "Hear Us" exhibit

5 Stained-glass windows

6 Doric Hall

7 Hall of Flags

8 Nurses Hall

9 Sacred Cod

10 State House Pine Cone

The Sacred Cod was bestowed on the House of Representatives by Boston merchant Jonathan Rowe. This carved fish has presided over the Commonwealth's legislators since 1784, though it vanished briefly in 1933, when Harvard's *Lampoon* magazine orchestrated a dastardly "codnapping" prank.

Imposing facade of the Massachusetts State House

Museum of Science

With over 700 colorful, interactive displays designed to thrill and amaze the minds of kids and adults alike, it's little wonder that this is one of Boston's most-visited museums. Popular attractions include the jaw-dropping, dome-shaped IMAX® screen in the Mugar Omni Theater, the techno-fabulous Hall of Human Life, electrifying lightning demonstrations, and daily live science shows.

5 Hall of Human Life

Cutting-edge subjects such as genetically modified organisms (GMO), DNA sequencing, the function of the human body, and all sorts of medical and nutritional issues are explored in this hall **(left)**. Visitors are given anonymous barcoded wristbands that are used to record their responses to the topics covered.

1 To the Moon

This popular exhibit includes full-size replicas of the Apollo Command Module and the Lunar Module cockpit. Kids can climb into the pilots' seats and relive the first landing on the moon. Nearby models show the growth of space stations from Skylab and Mir to the International Space Station. Pieces of moon rock are on show as well.

2 Butterfly Garden

Visitors to this tropical greenhouse walk among clouds of brightly colored, fluttering butterflies from New England and around the world. Interactive displays and exhibits highlight fascinating butterfly facts including the four stages of a butterfly's life, plus the miracle of metamorphosis, and how they fly.

3 Colossal Fossil

Meet Cliff, one of only four nearly complete triceratops skeletons on display in the world. He looks pretty good considering he's 65 million years old. Discovered in North Dakota in 2004, Cliff measures 23 ft (7 m) from horn tip to tail, and his head alone weighs 800 lb (362 kg).

4 Discovery Center

Geared to children under eight, this colorful, fun, activity-filled center is all about stimulating young minds with a sense of exploration. The changing activities can include excavating artifacts, analyzing fingerprints, or creating slime with borax and school glue. Well-trained staff help children discover the fun of problem-solving.

6 Lightning!

This live-theater show explores the science of electricity. Its star is the world's largest air-insulated Van de Graaff generator **(above)**, which safely zaps out sizzling lightning bolts of up to 1 million volts.

7 Charles Hayden Planetarium
This high-tech planetarium brings the dazzling night sky to life, and presents shows that include a look at images sent back by NASA's latest space missions, exploration of celestial sights, and immersive music shows.

Key to Floor Plan
- Second floor
- First floor
- Lower floor

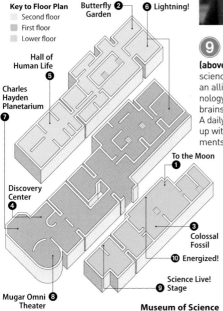

Butterfly ❷ Garden
❻ Lightning!
Hall of Human Life ❺
Charles Hayden Planetarium ❼
Discovery Center ❹
To the Moon ❶
❸ Colossal Fossil
❿ Energized!
Science Live! ❾ Stage
Mugar Omni ❽ Theater

Museum of Science

9 Science Live! Stage
This live presentation **(above)** features hands-on science demonstrations. Meet an alligator, explore nanotechnology, or find out why our brains fall for optical illusions. A daily changing schedule keeps up with the latest advancements making the news.

10 Energized!
Innovative exhibits cover the latest in alternative energy, including solar, wind, and hydroelectric power, and the solutions they can offer.

MUSEUM HISTORY
The Boston Museum of Science (MOS) traces its origins to the founding of the Boston Society of Natural History in 1830. The first permanent museum opened in 1864, making MOS one of the oldest science museums in America.

8 Mugar Omni Theater
This remarkable IMAX® Theater takes the "big-screen" concept into a whole new realm. Visitors sit below a 180-degree dome that fills their entire range of vision, immersing their senses with spectacular sights and powerful digital sounds.

NEED TO KNOW
MAP G3 ■ 1 Science Park ■ 617 723 2500 ■ "T" station: Science Park (green line) ■ www.mos.org

Open 9am–5pm Sat–Thu, 9am–9pm Fri

Adm adults $28; seniors $24; children (aged 3–11) $23

An extra fee is charged for admission to several attractions, including the Charles Hayden Planetarium, the 4D Theater, the Mugar Omni Theater and the Butterfly Garden. Individual admission to these attractions ranges from $6 to $10.

■ The museum's Riverview Café (situated on level 1, by the Museum Store) features several food stations, including a burger grill, a grab-and-go cooler of prepared sandwiches, a Starbucks coffee kiosk, and a "hearth" area that prepares macaroni and cheese, pizzas, and salads. Large groups visiting the Museum of Science can call ahead to arrange customised meals.

⭐ Boston Common and Public Garden

Verdant Boston Common has hosted auctions, festivals, cattle grazing, and public hangings over its almost 400-year history. The adjacent Public Garden, opened in 1839, was the US's first botanical garden. The French-style flowerbeds may only bloom in warmer months, but the garden exudes charm year-round, with its weeping willows and swan boats. The latter became an iconic image of Boston almost as soon as the first fleet glided onto the garden's pool in 1877.

1 Frog Pond
During summer, children splash under the iridescent spray of the pond's fountains (above). Come winter, Bostonians of all ages take to the ice. Skate rentals and delicious hot chocolate are nearby.

2 Lagoon Bridge
This elegant 1869 faux suspension bridge crossing the lagoon has served as the romantic setting for many wedding photos.

Make Way for Ducklings Statuettes 3
Eight little ducklings seem to have sprung from the pages of Robert McCloskey's much-loved kids' book and fallen in line behind their mother (right) at the lagoon's edge.

4 Shaw Memorial
Augustus Saint-Gaudens' lifelike bronze pays homage to the "Fighting 54th" – one of the only entirely African American regiments in the Civil War. Led by Boston-born Robert Shaw, the 54th amassed an impressive battle record.

5 Bronze of George Washington
The nation's first president cuts a stately figure at the western end of the Public Garden. Local sculptor Thomas Ball's 1869 bronze was an early horseback depiction of Washington.

6 Soldiers and Sailors Monument
Over 25,000 Union Army veterans remembered their fallen Civil War comrades at the 1877 dedication of Martin Milmore's impressive memorial. Bas-reliefs depict the soldiers' and sailors' departure to and return from war.

Boston Common and Public Garden

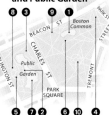

9 Founders' Memorial

John F. Paramino's 1930 bronze depicts William Blaxton, Boston's first English settler, greeting John Winthrop *(see p44)* as two Native Americans look on. The Massachusett people who lived in Boston left the city before Blaxton arrived.

7 Swan Boats

Summer hasn't officially arrived in Boston until the swan boats **(above)** emerge from hibernation and glide onto the Public Garden lagoon. With their gracefully arched necks and brilliantly painted bills, each swan can accommodate up to 20 people.

10 Parkman Bandstand

Built in 1912 to honor George Parkman, a benefactor of the park, this elegant bandstand **(left)** is modeled on Versailles' *Temple d'Amour* (temple of love). It hosts everything from concerts to political rallies.

8 Ether Monument

This 1868 statue commemorates a groundbreaking operation conducted under general anesthesia by ether at Massachusetts General Hospital in 1846 *(see p51)*. This is a rare monument to the powers of a drug.

EMERALD NECKLACE

Boston Common and Public Garden may seem like solitary urban oases, but they are two links in a greater chain of green space that stretches all the way through Boston to Roxbury. The Emerald Necklace, as this chain is called, was completed in 1896 by Frederick Law Olmsted, the man behind New York's Central Park.

NEED TO KNOW

MAP M4, N4
■ Bounded by Beacon, Park, Tremont, Arlington, & Boylston Sts ■ "T" station: Park Street (red/green line), Boylston & Arlington (both green line)

Boston Common Visitor Center: 139 Tremont St; 617 426 3115; open 8:30am–5pm Mon–Fri, 9am–5pm Sat & Sun (shorter weekend hours in winter)

Boston Parks & Recreation: 617 635 4505; www.boston. gov/departments/ parks-and-recreation

Swan Boats: 617 522 1966; open early-Apr– Sep: 10am–4pm daily; adm $4; www.swan boats.com

■ Food court-style quick bites such as sandwiches, burgers, and pizzas can be had at the Frog Pond Café.

■ The Commonwealth Shakespeare Company *(see p71)* stages free performances during the summer months.

TOP10 ⭐ Harvard University

America's most prestigious university – founded in 1636 and named for its earliest benefactor, John Harvard, in 1638 – has nurtured, tortured, and tickled some of the greatest minds of recent times. It has hosted everything from global economic summits to psychedelic drug experiments, and educated future US presidents and talk-show hosts. Visitors craving contact with the Harvard mystique are in luck – much of the university is open to the public.

1 Massachusetts Hall

Constructed in 1720, the university's oldest building was once a barrack for 640 revolutionary soldiers. The hall houses the office of the President of Harvard and is usually the center of protests against university policies.

2 John Harvard Statue

The inscription "John Harvard, Founder 1638" conceals three deceptions, hence its nickname "The Statue of Three Lies." First, there is no known portrait of John Harvard, so the sculptor used a model; second, Harvard did not found the university – it was named after him; and third, it was founded in 1636, not 1638.

3 Memorial Hall

Built over 8 years, Harvard's Memorial Hall **(above)** to its fallen Union army alumni was officially opened in 1878. Conceived as a multi-purpose building, it has hosted theatrical performances, graduation exercises, and assemblies of many other kinds.

4 Museum of Natural History

The exhibits at this museum (see p123) include George Washington's taxidermied pheasants, the Brazilian amethyst geode, the mounted Kronosaurus skeleton, and glass flowers – 850 species of plants, painstakingly replicated in colorful glass **(above)**.

5 Harvard Yard

Harvard's mixed residential and academic yard became the standard by which most American institutions of higher learning modeled their campuses.

6 Harry Widener Memorial Library

The Widener is the largest university library in the US. It houses an extremely impressive collection of rare books, including a Gutenberg Bible and early editions of Shakespeare's collected works.

Harvard University

9 Harvard Art Museums

Harvard's three art museums (see p123) were brought under one roof in a Renzo Piano building in 2014. It displays works **(above)** from Fogg Museum's world-class collection of European and American art, Germanic art holdings of the Busch-Reisinger Museum, and Asian collections of the Sackler Museum.

10 Science Center Plaza

This plaza in front of the Undergraduate Science Center is Harvard's busiest social space, featuring the Tanner Fountain, benches, and food trucks.

7 Semitic Museum

Founded in 1889, this museum houses more than 40,000 objects from excavations in Egypt, Iraq, Israel, Jordan, Syria, and Tunisia.

8 Peabody Museum of Archaeology & Ethnology

With an extensive collection, this museum (see p123) features a permanent Mesoamerica exhibit, Encounters with the Americas **(below)** exploring Latin American culture, and an exhibition devoted to canoes created by the Penobscot tribe of Maine.

HARVARD LAMPOON

Lampooners have made you laugh more than you might ever know. Aside from *The Harvard Lampoon* being the world's oldest humor magazine, nearly every successful contemporary American comedy to reach a television or movie screen boasts an ex-Lampooner on its writing staff. Well-known ex-Lampooners include the popular late night TV host Conan O'Brien.

NEED TO KNOW

MAP B1–C1 ■ "T" station: Harvard (red line) ■ www.harvard.edu; www.cambridgeusa.org

Harry Widener Memorial Library: Harvard Yard; 617 495 2413; book tour 2–3pm Thu; access only if accompanied by someone with valid Harvard ID

Semitic Museum: 6 Divinity Ave; 617 495 4631; open 11am–4pm Sun–Fri

■ Maps and free campus tours available from Smith Campus Center (1350 Massachusetts Ave; 617 495 1573).

■ Students refuel at Blackbird Doughnuts café inside the Smith Center (11 Holyoke St; 617 482 9000).

■ Harvard Film Archive, Carpenter Center, screens art and documentary films most nights (24 Quincy St; 617 495 4700).

Harvard Alumni

1 John Adams (1735–1826)
The nation's second president, although nervous upon entering the illustrious college as a freshman, eventually became enthralled by his studies.

2 Henry James (1843–1916)
The master of the psychological novel sourced plenty of material at Harvard for his scathing 1886 work *The Bostonians*.

3 W. E. B. Du Bois (1868–1963)
Founder of the National Association for the Advancement of Colored People (NAACP), Du Bois studied philosophy here, and said of his experience, "I was in Harvard, but not of it."

4 Franklin Delano Roosevelt (1882–1945)
Apparently more of a social butterfly than a dedicated academic, F.D.R. played pranks, led the freshman football squad, edited the *Harvard Crimson*, and earned a C average at Harvard before going on to become the 32nd President of the US.

5 T. S. Eliot (1885–1965)
The modernist poet of *The Waste Land* fame contributed much of his early work to the *Advocate* journal. He went on to edit many of those submissions for later publication.

6 John F. Kennedy (1917–63)
A barely average student but a good athlete, John F. Kennedy ran for President of the Freshman Class in 1936, and lost badly. He did rather well in 1960 when he became the 35th President of the United States.

Bernstein conducting an orchestra

7 Leonard Bernstein (1918–90)
The country's greatest composer and conductor was firmly grounded in the arts at Harvard. He edited the *Advocate* – the college's estimable literary and performing arts journal.

8 Benazir Bhutto (1953–2007)
This class of 1973 alumna later became the first woman to lead a modern Muslim state when she was elected prime minister of Pakistan in 1988. She was assassinated in 2007.

9 Bill Gates (b. 1955)
William Henry Gates III dropped out of Harvard in his third year to found Microsoft. He was made an Honorary Knight Commander of the Order of the British Empire (KBE) by Queen Elizabeth II in 2005 for his humanitarian and philanthropic work. He was also awarded an honorary doctorate in 2007 by Harvard.

Bill Gates

10 Barack Obama (b. 1961)
The 44th President of the United States attended Harvard Law School from 1988–91. His election as the first Black president of the *Harvard Law Review* gained extensive media attention.

HARVARD'S "ARCHITECTURAL ZOO"

Modernist architect James Stirling described Harvard as an "architectural zoo" – a well-deserved moniker as the campus seems to include buildings designed by every prominent architect of the last 200 years. Stirling himself designed the modernist 1985 Sackler Museum building *(see p123)*. Charles Bulfinch, whose claim to fame is the Massachusetts State House *(see p12)*, contributed the 1814 University Hall, featuring an ingenious granite staircase that supports the building by virtue of its inter-locking steps. Walter Gropius, the Bauhaus founder and Harvard architecture professor (1937–52), designed the Harvard Graduate Center in 1950, as well as several dormitory complexes. Gropius strove to make his modernist projects seem welcoming for inhabitants, but industrial finishes have not always resonated with succeeding generations. Le Corbusier's Carpenter Center for the Visual Arts is a lyrical collection of forms, materials, and innovative curves, with entire walls made of glass and deeply grooved concrete.

TOP 10
HARVARD'S BUILDINGS

1 Memorial Hall, 45 Quincy St (Ware and Van Brunt, 1878)

2 Loeb Drama Center, 64 Brattle St (Hugh Stebbins, 1959)

3 Massachusetts Hall, Harvard Yard (University Overseers, 1720)

4 Sackler Museum building, 485 Broadway (James Stirling, 1985)

5 Harvard Art Museums, 32 Quincy St (Renzo Piano and Payette, 2014)

6 University Hall, Harvard Yard (Charles Bulfinch, 1814)

7 Sever and Austin halls, Harvard Yard and North Yard (H. H. Richardson, 1880 and 1883)

8 Harvard Graduate Center, North Yard (Walter Gropius, 1950)

9 Carpenter Center for the Visual Arts, 24 Quincy St (Le Corbusier, 1963)

10 Undergraduate Science Center, Oxford St (Josep Lluís Sert, 1971)

Sever Hall and Austin Hall were designed by architect and 1859 Harvard alumnus H. H. Richardson. Both halls echo the distinctive Romanesque Revival style of his Copley Square masterpiece – Trinity Church *(see pp32–3)*.

Carpenter Center for Visual Arts, designed by Le Corbusier

TOP 10 ★ Around Newbury Street

Don't let the profusion of Prada-clad shoppers fool you: there's much more to elegant Newbury Street than world-class retail, people-watching, and alfresco dining. One of the first streets created on the marshland once known as Back Bay, Newbury has seen myriad tenants and uses over the past 150 years. Look closely and you'll glimpse a historical side to Newbury Street all but unseen by the fashionistas.

3 Church of the Covenant

English-born architect Richard Upjohn left his Neo-Gothic mark on Boston with the Church of the Covenant **(left)**, erected in 1865. It has the world's largest collection of Tiffany stained-glass.

4 Kingsley Montessori School

Built as a Spiritualist temple in 1884, this building became the dignified Exeter Street Theater in 1914. In 2005, it was converted to a private school.

1 Emmanuel Church

Architect Alexander Estey's impressive church (1860) was the first building to grace Newbury after the infilling of Back Bay. The adjacent Lindsey Chapel (1924) is home to the renowned Emmanuel Music ensemble.

2 French Cultural Center

Housed in a grand Back Bay mansion, the French Cultural Center hosts everything from lectures in French to concerts and a tasteful Bastille Day celebration. It also runs year-round courses in French for all ages.

5 New England Historic Genealogical Society

Members seek to discover more about their New England progenitors in one of the most extensive genealogical libraries in the US.

6 234 Berkeley St

Originally a natural history museum opened in 1864, this landmark building is now a high-end home furnishings store.

7 Commonwealth Avenue

A mall running along the center of Commonwealth Avenue *(see p88)* provides a leafy respite from the Newbury Street throngs. Benches and historical sculptures **(left)** line the pedestrian path.

⑨ Gibson House Museum

One of Back Bay's first private homes, Gibson House **(left)** was also one of the most modern residences of its day *(see p88)*. With its gas lighting, indoor plumbing, and heating, it spurred a building boom in the area.

BACK BAY'S ORIGINS

Since its settlement by Europeans, Boston has been reshaped to suit the needs of its inhabitants. Back Bay derives its name from the tidal swampland on which the neighborhood now stands. During the 19th century, gravel was used to fill the marsh and create the foundations for the grand avenues and picturesque brown-stone buildings that now distinguish this sought-after area.

Shops on Newbury Street

⑩ Boston Architectural College

For more than 125 years, aspiring architects have studied at this college **(below)**. The McCormick Gallery hosts a number of changing exhibitions.

⑧ Trinity Church Rectory

H. H. Richardson, principal architect of Trinity Church *(see pp32–3)*, was commissioned to build this rectory in 1879. His work echoes the Romanesque Revival style of the Copley Square church.

NEED TO KNOW

MAP K5, L5, M5 ■ "T" station: Arlington, Copley, or Hynes

Emmanuel Church: 15 Newbury St

French Cultural Center: 53 Marlborough St; 617 912 0400; open 9am–9pm Mon–Thu, 9am–5pm Fri; longer hours in summer

Church of the Covenant: 67 Newbury St

Kingsley Montessori School: 26 Exeter St; closed to the public

New England Historic Genealogical Society: 101 Newbury St; 617 536 5740; call ahead for schedule of free tours

Trinity Church Rectory: 233 Clarendon St; closed to the public

Boston Architectural College: 320 Newbury St; 617 585 0100; open 8am–10:30pm Mon–Fri, 8am–8pm Sat & Sun

■ Buy picnic supplies at **Deluca's Back Bay Market** *(239 Newbury St)*.

■ View the schedule for **Emmanuel Music at www. emmanuelmusic.org.**

Following pages Boston lit up at dusk

TOP 10 ⭐ Museum of Fine Arts, Boston

Since it was founded in 1870, the MFA has collected around 500,000 pieces from an array of cultures and civilizations, ranging from ancient Egyptian tomb treasures to stylish modern artworks. In 2010, the museum opened its long-anticipated Art of the Americas wing, designed by Norman Foster, which displays works created in North, Central, and South America.

5 Sargent Murals

Having secured some of John Singer Sargent's most important portraiture in the early 20th century, the MFA went one step further and commissioned the artist to paint murals and bas-reliefs on its central rotunda and colonnade. They feature gods and heroes from classical mythology.

1 The Fog Warning

This late 19th-century painting by Winslow Homer is part of a series in which the artist portrayed the difficult lives of the local fishers and their families. The painting depicts a fisherman trying to return to his vessel.

3 Egyptian Royal Pectoral

An extremely rare chest ornament **(above)**, this pectoral is nearly 4,000 years old. A vulture with a cobra on its left wing is depicted, poised to strike.

6 Dance at Bougival

This endearing image (1883) of a young couple dancing is one of the most beloved of Renoir's works. It exemplifies the artist's knack for taking a timeless situation and making it contemporary by dressing his subjects in the latest fashions.

4 Silverwork by Paul Revere

Famed for his midnight ride, Revere (see p44) was also known for his masterful silverwork **(left)**. The breadth of his ability is apparent in the museum's magnificent 200-piece collection.

2 John Singleton Copley Portraits

Self-taught and Boston-born Copley gained fame by painting the most affluent and influential Bostonians of his day, including figures like John Hancock, US President John Adams, and Isaac Winslow – depicted here **(right)** with his wife.

8 La Japonaise
Claude Monet's 1876 portrait **(left)** reflects a time when Japanese culture fascinated Europe's most style-conscious circles. The model, interestingly, is Monet's wife, Camille.

9 Japanese Temple Room
With its wood paneling and subdued lighting, the Temple Room evokes ancient Japanese shrines atop mist-enshrouded mountains. The statues, which date from as early as the 7th century, depict prominent figures from Buddhist texts.

10 Statue of King Aspelta
This statue **(right)** of the 6th-century BC Nubian king, Aspelta, was recovered in 1920 at Nuri in present-day Sudan during a Museum of Fine Arts/ Harvard joint expedition.

7 Christ in Majesty with Symbols
Acquired in 1919 from a small Spanish church, this medieval fresco had an amazingly complex journey to Boston, which involved waterproofing it with lime and parmesan for safe transportation.

NEED TO KNOW

MAP D6 ■ 465 Huntington Ave (Ave of the Arts) ■ 617 267 9300 ■ "T" station: Museum (green line/E train) ■ www.mfa.org

Open 10am–5pm Sat–Tue, 10am–10pm Wed–Fri

Adm adults $25; youth (aged 7–17) $10; under 6s free

■ The MFA has many restaurants and cafés, varying in formality and price, which are ideal for a drink or a quick bite.

■ On weekends, the MFA's Family Art Cart in the Shapiro Family Courtyard provides activities and materials to use in the galleries. Consult the museum's website for a full schedule of events.

■ Admission to the museum on Wednesdays 4–9:45pm is by voluntary donation.

Gallery Guide
European, Classical, Asian, and Egyptian art and artifacts occupy the original MFA building.

The Visitor Center is located on Level 1. The Linde Family Wing for Contemporary Art, on the west side of the museum, also houses the museum shop, cafés, and a restaurant. Arts from the Americas are spread across four levels in the Art of the Americas wing, on the east side of the museum. The wing has 49 galleries, plus a state-of-the-art auditorium, and displays over 5,000 works of art.

Museum of Fine Arts Collections

1 Art of Asia

For Asian art connoisseurs, the museum offers a dizzying overview of Japan's multiple artistic forms. In fact, the MFA holds the largest collection of ancient Japanese art outside of Japan. In addition to the tranquil Temple Room (see p29), with its centuries-old Buddhist statues, visitors should look out for the beautiful hanging scrolls and woodblock prints, with their magical, dramatic landscapes and spirited renderings of everyday life. Kurasawa fans, meanwhile, will be enthralled by the menacing samurai weaponry. Additionally, the Art of Asia collection contains exquisite objects from 2,000 years of Chinese, Indian, and Southeast Asian history, including sensuous ivory figurines, pictorial carpets, and vibrant watercolors.

Stuart woman's doublet, dating from 1610–15

2 Textile and Fashion Arts

Rotating displays highlight pictorial quilts, period fashions, fine Persian rugs, and pre-colonial Andean weavings. Particularly interesting are the textiles and costumes from the Elizabethan and Stuart periods – an unprecedented 1943 donation from the private collection of Elizabeth Day McCormick.

3 Classical Art

The remarkable Classical Art collection has a hoard of gold bracelets, glass, mosaic bowls, and stately marble busts. One of the earliest pieces is a c. 1500 BC gold axe, inscribed with symbols from a still-undeciphered Cretan language.

4 Art of the Americas

The MFA's Art of the Americas wing, designed by Norman Foster, opened in 2010. The wing features pieces dating from pre-Columbian times, through to the third quarter of the 20th century, and showcases about 5,000 works produced in North, Central, and South America. The museum has profited from generous benefactors over the years and the collection holds the world's finest ensemble of colonial New England furniture, rare 17th-century American portraiture, a superb display of American silver, and paintings by the country's own "Old" Masters, including Copley, Stuart, Cole, Sargent, Cassat, Homer, and many others.

5 Art of Egypt, Nubia, and the Ancient Near East

This collection is a treasure trove of millennia-old Egyptian sarcophagi, tomb finds, and Nubian jewelry and

Japan "Golden Age" (1781–1801) print

Egyptian mummy mask (AD 1–50)

objects from everyday life. The assemblage of Egyptian funerary pieces, including beautifully crafted jewelry and ceramic urns, is quite awe-inspiring. Ancient Near Eastern objects, with their bold iconography and rich materials, illustrate why the region is known as the Cradle of Civilization.

6 European Art to 1900

From 12th-century tempera baptism paintings to Claude Monet's *Haystacks*, the MFA's European collection is staggeringly diverse. Painstakingly transferred medieval stained-glass windows, beautifully illuminated bibles, and delicate French tapestries are displayed alongside works by Old Masters: Titian, El Greco, Rembrandt, and Rubens. A superlative Impressionist and Post-Impressionist collection boasts masterpieces from the likes of Renoir, Degas, Cézanne, and Van Gogh, plus the finest group of Monet's works outside of Paris.

La Berceuse (1889) by Van Gogh

7 Contemporary Art

Given Boston's affinity for the traditional, you might be surprised by this world-class collection of contemporary and late 20th-century art. It includes works by the painter and photographer Chuck Close and the Abstract Expressionist artist Jackson Pollock, which are on display in the Art of the Americas wing. New Media is also well-represented here.

Conch shell trumpet

8 Musical Instruments

Priceless 17th-century guitars, ornately inlaid pianos, and even a mouth organ are on view to visitors of the MFA. Among the more distinctive pieces is a c. 1796 English grand piano – the earliest extant example of a piano with a six-octave range – and a 1680 French guitar by the Voboam workshop.

9 Art of Africa and Oceania

Pre-colonial artifacts from these collections include Melanese canoe ornaments, dramatic Congolese bird sculptures and African funerary art. The most popular African displays are the powerful-looking 19th- and 20th-century wooden masks.

10 "Please be Seated!" Installations

View (and sit on) one of the country's most comprehensive collections of American contemporary furniture. The museum enourages visitors to admire and sit on these furniture pieces, so take a break and have a seat on fine American handiwork by designers such as Maloof, Castle, and Eames.

🔟⭐ Trinity Church

Boston has a great knack for creating curious visual juxtapositions, and one of the most remarkable is in Copley Square, where Henry Hobson Richardson's 19th-century Romanesque Revival Trinity Church reflects in the sleek, blue-tinted glass of the decidedly 20th-century 200 Clarendon Tower nearby. The breathtakingly beautiful church was named a National Historic Landmark in 1970 and has earned the distinction of being listed among the American Institute of Architects' ten greatest buildings in the country.

Burne-Jones Windows

Edward Burne-Jones' windows **(right)** – on the Boylston Street side – were inspired by the burgeoning English Arts and Crafts Movement. Its influence is readily apparent in his *David's Charge to Solomon*, with its bold patterning and rich colors.

2 The Foundation

As part of Richardson's daring plan, the first of 4,500 wooden support pilings for the church was driven into the soggy Back Bay landfill in 1873. Reverend Phillips Brooks laid the cornerstone two years later.

3 Central Tower

The church's central tower borrows its square design from the New Cathedral of Salamanca, in Spain. On the interior, vibrant wall paintings by La Farge depicting biblical figures hang in sharp contrast to the normally austere church interiors of the artist's day.

4 Front Facade and Side Towers

The Romanesque church of St Trophime in Arles, France, was Richardson's inspiration when he redesigned Trinity's front portico, along with its two new side towers **(left)**. The additions were put in place by his firm of architects in the 1890s, after his death in 1886.

Interior of Trinity Church

5 Embroidered Kneelers

Trinity's colorful kneelers have been stitched by parishioners in memory of people and events past. They serve as an informal folk history of the congregation.

6 Pulpit Carving

Preachers from throughout the ages, including St. Paul, Martin Luther, and Phillips Brooks of Trinity, are depicted in high relief on the pulpit designed by Charles Coolidge.

Phillips Brooks' Bust ⑦
Keeping watch over the baptismal font is Rector Brooks **(right)**. Renowned for his bold sermons, he was a rector at Trinity from 1869–91.

⑧ The Shop at Trinity
In addition to religious books and items, the store sells works inspired by the decorative details inside the church.

TRINITY SINGS "HALLELUJAH"

One of Boston's most cherished traditions is the singing of Handel's *Messiah*, with its unmistakable and rousing "Hallelujah Chorus," at Trinity during the Christmas season. Hundreds pack the sanctuary to experience the choir's ethereal, masterful treatment of the piece. Call 617 536 0944 for performance information.

⑩ Organ Pipes
The beautiful organ pipes frame the church's west wall. Exquisitely designed, ornately painted, and – of course – extremely sonorous, the pipes seem to hug the church's ceiling arches.

Trinity Church

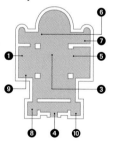

⑨ La Farge Windows
A newcomer to stained glasswork at the time, John La Farge approached his commissions, such as the breathtaking *Christ in Majesty*, with the same sense of daring and vitality that architect Richardson employed in his Trinity design.

NEED TO KNOW

MAP L5 ■ 206 Clarendon St ■ 617 536 0944 (church) ■ "T" station: Copley Sq (green line) & Back Bay (orange line) ■ www.trinitychurchboston.org

Church: open 10am–4:30pm Tue–Sat, after services–4:30pm Sun (for self-guided, audio, and guided tours); adm $10

Shop: open 10am–4:30pm Tue–Sat, after services–4:30pm Sun

■ Dine at Eataly *(see p93)* or the Prudential Center food court (800 Boylston St).

■ From September to June organ recitals are held every Friday, 12:15–12:45pm.

■ Guided tours of the church begin in the Welcome Center inside the Copley Square entrance.

■ Additionally, a free guided tour is offered every Sunday following the last morning service.

🔟 ⭐ Isabella Stewart Gardner Museum

One needn't be a patron of the arts to be wowed by the Gardner Museum. Its namesake traveled tirelessly to acquire a world-class art collection, which is housed in a Venetian-style palazzo where flowers bloom, sculpted nudes pose in hidden corners, and entire ceilings reveal their European origins. The palace is complemented by a striking modern building, designed by Renzo Piano, which holds an intimate performance hall, galleries, and a charming café.

② Titian Room
The most artistically significant gallery was conceived by Gardner as the palazzo's grand reception hall. It has an Italian flavor and show-cases Cillini's *Bindo Altoviti* **(left)** and Titian's *Rape of Europa*, one of the most important paintings inspired by Ovid's *Metamorphoses*.

The Courtyard ③
Gardner integrated Roman, Byzantine, Romanesque, Renaissance, and Gothic elements in the magnificent courtyard **(right)**, which is out of bounds for visitors but can be viewed through the graceful arches surrounding it.

① Long Gallery
Roman sculptural fragments and busts line glass cases that are filled with unusual 15th- and 16th-century books and artifacts. One such rare tome is a 1481 copy of Dante's *The Divine Comedy*, which features drawings by Botticelli.

④ Tapestry Room
Restored to its original 1914 state, this sweeping gallery houses two 16th-century Belgian tapestry cycles: one depicting *Scenes from the Life of Cyrus the Great* and the other *Scenes from the Life of Abraham*.

⑤ Dutch Room
Housing some of Gardner's most impressive Dutch and Flemish paintings, this room lost a Vermeer and three Rembrandts in a 1990 art heist that still remains unsolved.

⑥ Macknight, Yellow, and Blue Rooms
The Macknight, Yellow and Blue rooms **(left)** house portraits and sketches by Gardner's contemporaries such as, Manet, Matisse, Degas, and Sargent. Of particular note is Sargent's *Mrs Gardner in White*.

7 Gothic Room
John Singer Sargent's masterful and revealing 1888 portrait of Mrs Gardner **(left)** is here, as well as medieval liturgical artwork from the 13th century.

8 Veronese Room
With its richly gilded and painted Spanish-leather wall-coverings, it's easy to miss this gallery's highlight: look up at Paolo Veronese's 16th-century master-work *The Coronation of Hebe*.

FENWAY COURT

Before Isabella Stewart Gardner died in 1924 she stipulated in her will that her home and her collection become a public museum. She believed that works of art should be displayed in a setting that would fire the imagination. So the collection, exhibited over three floors, is arranged purely to enhance the viewing of the individual treasures. To encourage visitors to respond to the artworks themselves, many of the 2,500 objects – from ancient Egyptian pieces to Matisse's paintings – are left unlabeled, as Gardner had requested.

Isabella Stewart Gardner Museum

Key to Floor Plan
- First floor
- Second floor
- Third floor

NEED TO KNOW

MAP D6 ■ 25 Evans Way ■ 617 566 1401 ■ "T" station: Museum (green line/E train) ■ www.gardnermuseum.org

Open 11am–5pm Wed–Mon (to 9pm Thu)

Adm $13–20; free for anyone named Isabella

■ Light salads and sandwiches are served in the museum's café.

■ The museum's Calderwood Hall hosts classical as well as contemporary music concerts. Check website for details.

■ On the third Thursday of every month, the museum hosts creative studio projects as well as live music, dance and performance art.

9 Spanish Cloister
With stunning mosaic tiling and a Moorish arch, the Spanish Cloister looks like a hidden patio at the Alhambra. But Sargent's sweeping *El Jaleo* (1882), all sultry shadows and rich hues, gives the room its distinctiveness.

10 Raphael Room
Gardner was the first collector to bring works by Raphael to the US; three of his major works are here, alongside Botticelli's *Tragedy of Lucretia* and Crivelli's *St. George Slaying the Dragon*.

TOP10 ⭐ Charlestown Navy Yard

Some of the most storied battleships in American naval history began life at Charlestown Navy Yard. Established in 1800 as one of the country's first naval yards, Charlestown remained vital to US security until its decommissioning in 1974. From the wooden-hulled USS *Constitution* built in 1797 to the World War II steel destroyer USS *Cassin Young*, the yard gives visitors an all-hands-on-deck historical experience unparalleled in America.

1 USS Constitution

First tested in action during the War of 1812, the USS *Constitution* **(above)** is the world's oldest warship still afloat. On July 4, a tugboat helps her perform an annual turnaround cruise.

2 Navy Yard Visitor Center

Begin your stroll through the yard at the National Park Service-operated Visitor Center, where you can pick up literature about the site's many attractions and check on tour schedules.

3 Bunker Hill Monument

This 220-ft (67-m) granite obelisk **(right)**, nearby, has towered over Charlestown since 1842. It was built to commemorate the first pitched battle of the American Revolution *(see p14)*.

4 USS Cassin Young

Never defeated, despite withstanding multiple kamikaze bomber-attacks in the Pacific, this World War II era destroyer **(right)** could be considered USS *Constitution's* 20th-century successor.

5 Commandant's House

The oldest building in the yard, dating from 1805, housed the commandants of the First Naval District. With its sweeping harbor views and wraparound veranda, this elegant mansion was ideal for entertaining dignitaries from all over the world.

6 Dry Dock #1

To facilitate hull repairs, Dry Dock #1 **(left)** was opened in 1833. It was drained by massive steam-powered pumps. USS *Constitution* was the first ship to be given an overhaul here.

7 Ropewalk

This quarter-mile- (0.5-km-) long building (1837) houses steam-powered machinery that produced rope rigging for the nation's warships.

8 USS Constitution Museum

With activities to keep kids entertained, as well as enough nautical trivia and artifacts – from muskets **(above)** to spoils of war – to satisfy a naval historian, this museum brings to life USS *Constitution's* two centuries of service.

9 Muster House

This octagonal brick building was designed in the Georgian-revival style popular in the northeast in the mid-19th century. The house served as an adminis-tration hub, where the yard's clerical work was carried out.

10 Marine Railway

The Navy Yard has constantly evolved to meet changing demands and developments. The marine railway was built in 1918 to haul submarines and other vessels out of the water for hull repairs.

Charlestown Navy Yard

OLD IRONSIDES

Given the boat's 25-inch- (63-cm-) thick hull at the waterline, it's easy to imagine why the USS *Constitution* earned its nickname "Old Ironsides." Pitted against HMS *Guerriere* during the War of 1812, the ship engaged in a shoot-out that left *Guerriere* all but destroyed. Seeing British cannon balls "bouncing" off USS *Constitution's* hull, a sailor allegedly exclaimed, "Huzzah! Her sides are made of iron." The rest is history.

NEED TO KNOW

MAP H2 ▪ "T" station: North Station (green & orange lines) ▪ Water shuttle from Long Wharf; www.mbta.com

Navy Yard Visitor Center: Building Number 5; 617 242 5601; opening hours vary, call to check; www.nps.gov/bost

Bunker Hill Monument, USS Cassin Young, USS Constitution: opening hours vary, check website for details; www.nps.gov/bost

USS Constitution Museum: open Apr–Oct: 9am–6pm daily; Nov–Mar: 10am–5pm daily; donation

▪ Try some pub grub at the atmospheric Warren Tavern *(2 Pleasant St).*

▪ Photo ID (18 and above) and metal screening required to board the USS *Constitution.*

TOP 10 ⭐ New England Aquarium

The sea pervades nearly every aspect of Boston life, so it's only appropriate that the New England Aquarium is one of the city's most popular attractions. What sets this aquarium apart from many similar institutions is its commitment not only to presenting an exciting environment to learn about marine life, but also to conserving the natural habitats of its thousands of gilled, feathered, and whiskered inhabitants.

① Penguin Exhibit

Two species of penguins – southern Rockhoppers and African – coexist here, frolicking on the central island and taking dips in the pool.

② Yawkey Coral Reef Center

At the top of the Giant Ocean Tank, this exhibit reveals a closeup look at species found inhabiting the coral reefs of the Caribbean, including long-spined sea urchins and gently swaying garden eels that burrow together in colonies.

⑤ Marine Mammal Center

Observe Northern fur seals as they frolic in an open-air exhibit at the edge of the Boston Harbor. Meet the seals **(above)** and sea lions face-to-face at the large observation deck.

③ Blue Planet Action Center

Interactive exhibits in this section focus on the aquarium's ecological missions: saving corals from climate change and acidification, protecting the critically endangered North Atlantic right whale, and promoting sustainable fishing practices.

④ Atlantic Harbor Seal Exhibit

Harbor seals **(below)** swim, feed, and play in specially designed tanks outside the aquarium. All have either been born in captivity or rescued and deemed unfit for release into the wild.

⑥ Indo-Pacific Coral Reef

Created in 2019, this immersive exhibit features floor-to-ceiling tanks filled with hand-painted artificial coral and brightly colored inhabitants such as blue-striped cleaner fish, unicorn tangs, and mandarinfish **(above)**.

7 Giant Ocean Tank

Displaying a spectacular four-story Caribbean reef, the Giant Ocean Tank (above) teems with sea turtles, sharks, moray eels, brightly colored tropical fish, and scores of other species in its 200,000-gallon (900,000-liter) space.

9 Whale Watch

The aquarium's whale watch catamarans, running mid-March to mid-November, offer a unique glimpse into the life cycles of the world's largest mammals. The swift boats voyage far outside Boston Harbor to the Stellwagen Bank, a prime feeding area for whales.

10 Gulf of Maine

This six-tank exhibit shows New England's marine and seashore environments inhabited by giant sea stars, sharp-clawed crustaceans, and cold water fish such as cod, halibut, and dogfish.

THE AQUARIUM'S MISSION

The aquarium's aim, first and foremost, is to inspire and support marine conservation. Its Marine Conservation Action Fund has fought on behalf of endangered marine animals worldwide, helping to protect humpback whales in the South Pacific, sea turtles in New England, and dolphins in Peru.

NEED TO KNOW

MAP R3 ■ Central Wharf ■ 617 973 5200 ■ "T" station: Aquarium (blue line) ■ www.neaq.org for general info, including current IMAX® features

Open 9am–5pm Mon–Fri, 9am–6pm Sat & Sun (extended hours Jul–Aug)

Adm adults $31; seniors $29; children (aged 3–11) $22; under 3s free

Whale Watch: 617 973 5206 for reservations and rate information

IMAX®: call 866 815 IMAX® (4629) for show times; adm adults $9.95; seniors $7.95; children (aged 3–11) $7.95

■ Enjoy the local catch at moderately priced **Legal Sea Foods Long Wharf** *(MAP R3; 255 State St)*, located on the harborfront. Quick bites can also be had at the Quincy Market food hall *(see p101)* nearby.

■ Purchase discount combo tickets for the aquarium along with an IMAX® film or a whale-watching excursion.

8 Science of Sharks

Wrap-around video screens and educational exhibits (above) introduce visitors to these fascinating creatures and their underwater world. This section of the aquarium also has some tanks containing smaller shark species.

Key to Floor Plan
- First floor
- Second floor
- Third floor

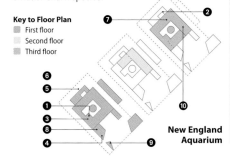

New England Aquarium

The Top 10
of Everything

**Northern Avenue Bridge
and skyscrapers**

Moments in History

Battle of Concord Bridge, 1775

1 1630: English Move to Boston

For centuries, the Massachusett people inhabited the area that is now Boston. In 1622–3, they abandoned the region after much of the population had succumbed to a plague. Under the leadership of John Winthrop (see p44), English Puritans moved here from Charlestown, naming this land Boston in honor of their English roots.

2 1636: Harvard Created

Boston's Puritan leaders established a college at Newtowne (later Cambridge) to educate future generations of clergy. When young Charlestown minister John Harvard died two years later and left his books and half his money to the college, it was renamed Harvard (see p20) in his memory.

Statue of *Art*, Boston Public Library

3 1775: American Revolution

Friction between colonists and the British Crown had been building for more than a decade when British troops marched on Lexington to confiscate rebel weapons. Forewarned by Paul Revere (see p44),

local militia, known as the Minute Men, skirmished with British regulars on Lexington Green. During the second confrontation at Concord, "the shot heard round the world" marked the beginning of the Revolution, which ended in American independence with the 1783 Treaty of Paris.

4 1845: Irish Arrived

Irish citizens, fleeing the devastating potato famine in their country, arrived in Boston in tens of thousands, many eventually settling in the south of the city. By 1900, the Irish were the dominant community in Boston. They flexed their political muscle accordingly, culminating in the election of John F. Kennedy (see p45) as president in 1960.

5 1848: Boston Public Library Founded

The Boston Public Library was established as the first publicly supported municipal library in the US. In 1895 the library moved into the Italianate "palace of the people" on Copley Square (see p87).

6 1863: Black Boston Went to War

Following decades of agitation to abolish slavery, the city sent the North's first African American regiment to join Union forces in the Civil War. The regiment was honored by the Shaw Memorial on Boston Common (see p18).

7 1897: Subway Opened

The Tremont Street subway, the first underground in the US, was opened on September 1 to ease road congestion. It cost $4.4 million to construct and the initial fare was five cents. The Massachusetts Bay Transportation Authority (MBTA) now transports 1.3 million people daily.

1958: Freedom Trail Opened

This historical walking tour *(see p12)* connects the city's sights. It was based on a 1951 *Boston Herald Traveler* column by William Scofield, and was the first of its kind in the US.

Zakim Bridge, part of the Big Dig

2007: The Big Dig

The $15 billion highway project to alleviate traffic congestion was completed in 2007, leaving in its place the Rose Kennedy Greenway Park and the soaring Zakim Bridge, one of the world's widest cable-stayed bridges.

Boston Marathon bombing tributes

10 2013: Boston Marathon Bombing

On April 15, 2013, two terrorist bombs exploded near the finish line of the Boston Marathon, killing three people and injuring 264. In 2019, a memorial of four bronze spires and granite markers was installed in two locations on Boylston Street to honor the victims.

TOP 10 INNOVATIONS

1 Sewing Machine
Elias Howe invented the sewing machine in Cambridge in 1845, but spent decades securing patent rights.

Howe's sewing machine

2 Surgical Anesthesia
Ether was used for the very first time to anesthetize patients at the Massachusetts General Hospital in 1846.

3 Telephone
Alexander Graham Bell invented the telephone in his Boston laboratory in 1876.

4 Safety Razor
Bostonian King Camp Gillette invented the safety razor with disposable blades in 1901.

5 Mutual Fund
Massachusetts Investors Trust opened in 1924 as the first modern mutual fund that pooled investors' money to purchase portfolio stocks.

6 Programmable Digital Computer
The first programmable digital computer, Mark 1, was built by a Harvard team in 1946. The 750,000 components of the computer weighed about 10,000 lb (454 kg).

7 Microwave Oven
A Raytheon company engineer placed popcorn in front of a radar tube in 1946 and discovered the principle behind the microwave oven.

8 Instant Film
Cambridge, Massachusetts, inventor Edwin Land devised the Polaroid camera, launched in 1948.

9 Email
Ray Tomlinson, an engineer at Bolt, Beranek, and Newman in Cambridge, sent the first email message in 1971.

10 Facebook
Harvard student Mark Zuckerberg posted the first message to Facemash (social network site Facebook's predecessor) in 2003.

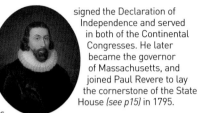 Figures in Boston's History

1 John Winthrop (1587–1649)

Acting on a daring plan put together by English Puritans in 1629, John Winthrop led approximately 800 settlers to the Americas to build a godly civilization in the wilderness. He settled his Puritan charges at Boston in 1630 (see p42) and served as governor of the Massachusetts Bay Colony until his death.

John Winthrop

2 Increase Mather (1639–1723)

Harvard-educated preacher Increase Mather solidified the hold of Puritan theologians on Massachusetts. When William III took the English Crown, Mather persuaded the king to grant a charter that gave the colony the right to elect the council of the governor in 1691. His influence was later undermined by his support of the 1692 Salem witch trials.

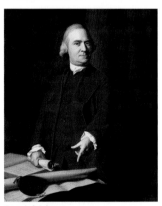

Samuel Adams

3 Samuel Adams (1722–1803)

Failed businessman Samuel Adams became Boston's master politician in the eventful years leading up to the Revolution (see p14). Adams signed the Declaration of Independence and served in both of the Continental Congresses. He later became the governor of Massachusetts, and joined Paul Revere to lay the cornerstone of the State House (see p15) in 1795.

4 Paul Revere (1735–1818)

Best known for his "midnight ride" to forewarn the rebels of the British march on Concord, Revere served the American Revolution as organizer, messenger, and propagandist. A gifted silversmith with many pieces in the Museum of Fine Arts (see pp28–31), he founded the metalworking firm that gilded the State House dome and sheathed the hull of the USS *Constitution*.

5 Harrison Gray Otis (1765–1848)

In the 1790s, Harrison Gray Otis and James Mason transformed Beacon Hill from a hilly pasture into a chic neighborhood that embodies the Federal building style. Otis championed the architecture of Charles Bulfinch, and three of his Bulfinch-designed houses still grace Beacon Hill, including the one now known as Harrison Gray Otis House (see p82).

6 Donald McKay (1810–80)

McKay built the largest and swiftest of the great clipper ships in his East Boston shipyard in 1850. The speedy vessels revolutionized long-distance shipping at the time of the California gold rush and gave Boston its last glory days as a mercantile port before the rise of rail transportation.

7 Mary Baker Eddy (1821–1910)

After recovering from a major accident, Eddy wrote *Science and Health with Key to the Scriptures*, the basis of Christian Science. She founded a church in Boston in 1879, and in 1892 reorganized it as the First Church of Christ, Scientist *(see p88)*. Eddy also established the Pulitzer prize-winning *Christian Science Monitor* newspaper in 1908.

8 James Michael Curley (1874–1958)

Self-proclaimed champion of "the little people," Curley used patronage and Irish pride to retain a stranglehold on Boston politics from his election as mayor in 1914 until his defeat at the polls in 1949. Known as "the rascal king" he embodied political corruption but created many enduring public works.

James Michael Curley at a parade

9 John F. Kennedy (1917–63)

Grandson of Irish American mayor John "Honey Fitz" Fitzgerald and son of ambassador Joseph Kennedy, John F. Kennedy represented Boston in both houses of the US Congress before he became the first Roman Catholic elected president of the United States. The presidential library *(see p133)* at Columbia Point recounts the story of his brief, but intense, period in office.

10 Michelle Wu (1985–)

In a historic election in 2021, Michelle Wu was elected Mayor of Boston, making her the first person of color and woman elected to this office. In 2013, she had been elected to the office of Boston city Councillor. Wu is a graduate of Harvard University and Harvard Law School.

TOP 10 LITERARY BOSTONIANS

Acclaimed author Dorothy West

1 Anne Bradstreet (c. 1612–72)
America's first poet, Anne Bradstreet published *The Tenth Muse, Lately Sprung Up in America* in 1650.

2 Ralph Waldo Emerson (1803–82)
Poet and philosopher, Ralph Waldo Emerson espoused transcendentalism as well as pioneered American literary independence.

3 Henry Wadsworth Longfellow (1807–82)
Known for epic poems such as *Hiawatha*, Longfellow also translated Dante.

4 Louisa May Alcott (1832–88)
Little Women sealed the literary fame of Louisa May Alcott. She also served as a nurse in the Civil War.

5 Henry James (1843–1916)
Master of sonorous prose, Henry James is considered one of the creators of the psychological novel.

6 Dorothy West (1907–98)
African American novelist and essayist, Dorothy West made sharp observations about class and race conflicts.

7 Elizabeth Bishop (1911–79)
A poet and a short story writer, Bishop was known for her witty and expressive verse.

8 Robert Lowell (1917–77)
The "confessional poetry" of Robert Lowell went on to influence a whole generation of writers.

9 Robert Parker (1932–2010)
Scholar of mystery literature, Robert Parker is best known for his signature detective Spenser.

10 Dennis Lehane (b.1965)
Novelist Dennis Lehane brings a dark, tragic vision to the working-class neighborhoods of Boston.

🔟 Waterfront Areas

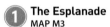
Sailing boats on the Charles River

① The Esplanade
MAP M3

Provided the Charles River Basin has not frozen over, collegiate rowing crews, canoeists, small sailboats, and the occasional coast guard patrol all share the waters off the Esplanade. Find a bench facing the water and take in the scene.

② Castle Island Reservation
2010 Day Blvd, South Boston
▪ **617 727 5290**

Connected to the mainland via an earthen causeway and crowned by the c. 1851 Fort Independence, Castle Island (see p132) is New England's oldest continually fortified site. Aside from exploring the fort's bunkers and tunnels (in season), visitors enjoy fine panoramic views of Boston Harbor.

③ Constitution Beach
Bennington St, East Boston

Views of Downtown don't get much better than those from this tastefully revitalized beach and park area in East Boston. A clean beach, picnic areas, and lifeguards make this a favorite with families.

④ Long Wharf
MAP R2

Long Wharf has been indispensable to Boston's merchant industry for over 300 years. Given the wharf's deep frontage and proximity to waterfront warehouses, the biggest ships of their day could dock here. Today, ferry services and cruise vessels depart from here, creating a spirited dock scene, and there's excellent waterside dining at a branch of the restaurant Legal Sea Foods.

⑤ Fish Pier

By 1926 – 12 years after its construction – the Greco-Roman style Commonwealth Pier (aka Fish Pier) had become the world's busiest and largest fish market. The day's catch is still brought to the early morning market here. Sample some of it in hearty chowders and the decadent dishes served in the city's seafood restaurants (see pp64–5).

⑥ Fort Point Channel
MAP H5

Fort Point has lured artists to the neighborhood with affordable studio space in old warehouse buildings. Open studios in May and October offer a peek inside and a chance to bag a bargain on artwork. Today, the neighborhood houses the $300-million Federal Courthouse and trendy cafés and restaurants.

Boats on the Fort Point Channel

⑦ Christopher Columbus Park
MAP P2

Featuring an Italian marble sculpture of the seafaring colonizer, Christopher Columbus Park is among the North End's best-kept secrets. Vine-covered arches, manicured gardens, and sweeping harbor and skyline views make this a place to linger.

Swanky Rowes Wharf

⑧ Rowes Wharf
MAP R3

Framed by the colossal atrium of the Boston Harbor Hotel (see p146), Rowes Wharf is a popular docking spot for the high-end harbor cruise outfits and is a luxurious contrast to the city's grittier, saltier working docks. The hotel sponsors free concerts and film screenings on summer evenings.

⑨ Langone Park
MAP H2

North End's Langone Park boasts supreme frontage on the harbor, looking out toward Charlestown. On warm days, the neighborhood's old guard comes here to enjoy a game of *bocce* (bowls). Nearby, kids play baseball or splash around in the outdoor pool.

⑩ Seaport District

This bustling waterfront development encompasses the historic shipping and fishing piers east of Fort Point Channel. Today, the area is a vibrant mix of hotels, bars, and entertainment.

TOP 10 SCENIC VIEWS

Serene Weeks Footbridge

1 Weeks Footbridge
MAP B2
A prime spectator spot during the Head of the Charles Regatta (see p73).

2 Longfellow Bridge
MAP M2
The entire Charles River Basin becomes your oyster on the "T" between Kendall and Charles/MGH stops.

3 Bunker Hill Monument
Climb the monument (see p36) to see the city laid out before you.

4 Spirit of Boston Cruises
World Trade Center ▪ 617 548 1450
Admire the city from the water as you enjoy brunch, lunch, drinks, or dinner.

5 Charlestown Bridge
MAP G2
This bridge offers splendid harbor and Downtown vistas.

6 John J. Moakley Courthouse Park
MAP H4
This beautiful waterfront park has fine views of the towering Financial District.

7 Hyatt Regency Cambridge
MAP C4 ▪ 575 Memorial Dr, Cambridge ▪ 617 492 1234
Gaze across the river from the seasonal patio at Zephyr on the Charles.

8 Independence Wharf Deck
The observation deck atop 470 Atlantic Ave has great views of Seaport District.

9 Dorchester Heights Monument
MAP Q3 ▪ 15 State S
The park around this commemorative spire offers broad views of the harbor.

10 Hyatt Regency Boston Harbor
101 Harborside Dr, East Boston
▪ 617 568 1234
The Hyatt's Harborside Grill and Patio boasts panoramic Boston views.

🔟 Boston Harbor Islands

1 Georges Island
Islands open mid-May–mid-Oct (information booth at Long Wharf) ■ 617 223 8666 ■ www.bostonharbor islands.org

As the terminal for the harbor islands ferry and water shuttles to other islands, Georges Island is the gateway to the Boston Harbor Islands National and State park, which includes 34 islands and mainland parks. Here, visitors can hike, explore historic buildings, bird-watch, and visit the Civil-War-era Fort Warren, where there's a snack bar and a gift shop. See the website for information on all Boston Harbor islands.

Visitors at Georges Island

2 Peddocks Island
Peddocks is one of Boston Harbor's largest and most diverse islands. Hiking trails circle a pond, salt marsh, and coastal forest, and pass by Fort Andrews, which was active in harbor defense from 1904 through to World War II. The island is known for the beach plums and wild roses that bloom profusely in the dunes. A visitor center and campsite make it an overnight destination.

3 Lovells Island
Known for its extensive dunes, Lovells also has an unsupervised swimming beach. Extensive hiking trails lead across the dunes and through woodlands. The remains of Fort Standish, which was active during the Spanish American War and World War I, can also be explored.

4 Grape and Bumpkin Islands
Both these islands are a delight for naturalists – Bumpkin for its wildflowers, raspberries, and bayberries, and Grape for its wild roses and bird life. On Bumpkin Island, hiking trails pass the ruins of a farmhouse and 19th-century children's hospital, which also housed German prisoners rescued from Boston Harbor in World War I and later polio patients, before burning down in 1945.

5 Deer Island
Accessed by a causeway from the mainland, part of the island was opened in 2006 for recreation and walking, and it offers dramatic views of the Boston skyline. Deer Island is also known for its impressive, state-of-the-art $3.8 billion sewage treatment plant. Distinguished by 12 gigantic egg-shaped digesters, it was key to cleaning up Boston Harbor.

6 Spectacle Island
Featuring some of the highest peaks of the harbor islands, the Spectacle Island has the best Boston skyline view. The construction of a café and visitor center has made it one of the most popular of all the harbor islands. Visitors can enjoy 5 miles (8 km) of trails, including an ADA Accessible Perimeter Trail, and swimming beaches with lifeguards.

The scenic Spectacle Island

Little Brewster Island, with its historic lighthouse

7 Little Brewster Island
Island closed due to storm damage, call for details ■ 617 223 8666 ■ Adm

Boston Light, the first US lighthouse, was constructed here in 1716 and it remains the last staffed offshore lighthouse in the country. Check www.bostonharborislands.org for the schedule of weekly cruises that sail past Boston Light and two other lighthouses.

8 Gallops Island
Once the site of a popular summer resort, Gallops also served as quarters for Civil War soldiers, including the Massachusetts 54th Regiment (see p18). The island has an extensive sandy beach, a picnic area, hiking paths, and historic ruins of a former quarantine and immigration station. The Massachusetts Department of Conservation and Recreation has closed the island indefinitely for a thorough environmental clean up.

9 Thompson Island
Open Jun–Aug: Sat & Sun ■ 617 328 3900 ■ Ferries depart from EDIC Pier off Summer Street ■ Adm

A learning center since the 1830s, Thompson is the site of an Outward Bound program serving more than 5,000 students annually. The island's diverse landscape includes rocky and sandy shores, a large salt marsh, sumac groves, and a hardwood forest. Herons, killdeer, and shorebirds abound.

10 World's End
Operated by Trustees of Reservations: 1 781 740 6665 ■ Adm for non-members

This 0.4-sq-mile (1-sq-km) peninsula overlooking Hingham Bay is a geological sibling of the Harbor Islands, with its two glacial drumlins, rocky beaches, ledges, cliffs, and both salt and freshwater marshes. Frederick Law Olmsted (see p19) laid out the grounds for a homestead development here in the late 19th century. The homes were never built, but carriage paths, formal plantings, and hedgerows remain. World's End is accessed by road via Hingham.

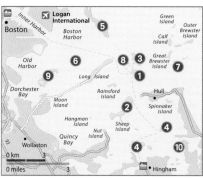

🔟 Off the Beaten Path

Sports Museum of New England

① Sports Museum of New England

MAP P1 ▪ TD Garden, 100 Legends Way ▪ 617 624 1234 ▪ Tours 10am–3pm Mon–Sat, 11am–3pm Sun; closed on event days, check website ▪ Adm ▪ www.sportsmuseum.org

Spread over two floors above the TD Garden, home of the Bruins (ice hockey) and Celtics (basketball), are displays on all the city's renowned teams. The collection includes a section of the wooden seats from the original Boston Garden, where you can watch screenings of historic games.

② ICA Watershed

Boston Harbor Shipyard & Marina, 256 Marginal St ▪ 617 478 3100 ▪ Open Jun–Aug: 10am–5pm Tue, Wed, Sat & Sun (to 9pm Thu & Fri) ▪ www.icaboston.org

The summer outpost of ICA (see p96) has innovative exhibitions and a permanent gallery. A free shuttle from ICA is available with a ticket purchase.

③ Captain Jackson's Historic Chocolate Shop

MAP Q1 ▪ Clough House, 21 Unity St ▪ 617 858 8231 ▪ Opening hours vary, check website for details ▪ www.oldnorth.com/captainjacksons

This shop explores the history of chocolate making during the American colonial period. Engaging demonstrations, conducted daily, illustrate how chocolate was produced in the 18th century. Visitors can also purchase chocolate blocks and coffee.

④ Mapparium

MAP K6 ▪ 200 Massachusetts Ave ▪ 617 450 7000 ▪ Tours 10:30am–4:40pm daily ▪ Adm ▪ www.marybakereddylibrary.org

The oddly fascinating Mapparium is a stained-glass globe the size of a large room that you view from the inside as you stroll through it along a glass walkway. Illuminated by LED lighting, the countries represented on the globe's surface are those that existed when it was built in 1935. Fabulous acoustics allow whispers to be heard at opposite ends of the space. The Mapparium is located in the Mary Baker Eddy Library, which also features a small museum dedicated to Eddy (see pp44–5) and the Christian Science religion she founded.

Stained-glass Mapparium

⑤ The New England Holocaust Memorial

MAP Q4 ▪ Between Congress and Union Sts

Six luminous glass towers soar above a black granite path bordered by lawns and trees. The structures represent the six main death camps and the six million Jews who died during the six years of World War II.

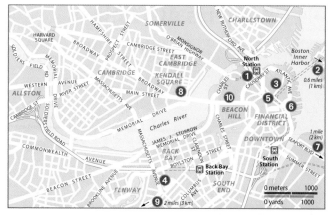

6 Ghosts and Gravestones
MAP R3 ■ 200 Atlantic Ave
■ 866 754 9136 ■ Adm ■ www.
ghostsandgravestones.com

Hop on the black trolley of doom
with a gravedigger guide for a
"frightseeing" tour of the city's
most haunted spots, and visit the
site of New England's greatest
grave-robbing scandal.

7 The Lawn on D
420 D St ■ 877 393 3393
■ Open dawn to dusk ■ www.
signatureboston.com/lawn-on-d

One of Boston's newest and most
popular green spaces, The Lawn on
D is located in the heart of the Seaport
District and is close to the Convention
and Exhibition Center. This hip outdoor space features live music, lawn
games, and food trucks.

8 Paddle the Charles River
MAP E3 ■ Charles River Canoe and
Kayak, Broad Canal Way, Kendall Sq,
Cambridge ■ 617 965 5110 ■ Adm
■ www.paddleboston.com

What better way to get a whole
new perspective on Boston than by
seeing it from the water? Visitors
can rent their own canoe, kayak,
or paddleboard or even join a tour
with a larger group. Options on
offer include Skyline, Sunset, and
Boston Harbor tours (by kayak only).

Interior of Samuel Adams Brewery

9 Samuel Adams Brewery
30 Germania St ■ 617 368
5080 ■ Tours: www.samadamsboston
brewery.com

This lively tour of the Samuel Adams
craft brewery takes you through the
process and offers free tastings of
Samuel Adams' famous beers. Note
that the tour tickets are sold on a
first-come-first-serve basis.

10 Paul S. Russell, MD Museum of Medical History and Innovation
MAP N2 ■ Massachusetts General
Hospital, 2 North Grove St ■ 617
724 8009 ■ Open 9am–5pm Mon–
Fri (Apr–Oct: 11am–5pm Sat)
■ www.massgeneral.org/museum

This museum traces medical innovation with displays, artifacts, and
guides. The Ether Dome, nearby,
was the site of the first successful
use of ether anesthetic in surgery.

🔟 Children's Attractions

Exhibit in the Children's Museum

① Children's Museum

This venerable funhouse *(see p96)* pioneered the interactive-exhibit concept now found in museums worldwide. It includes a climbing wall, a Big Dig-style *(see p43)* construction zone, and a science playground where tracks, balls, and bubbles encourage kids to investigate, and make learning fun. The museum runs a program of special events throughout the year covering a range of subjects, including health, engineering, and literacy.

Boston Duck Tours

② Museum of Science

Hands-on learning exhibits at this museum *(see pp16–17)*, such as assembling animal skeletons or building a computer model, teach children the thrill of discovery. The Omni Theater delights with its fast-paced IMAX® projections, while the planetarium places the cosmos within reach. There are also 4D film presentations and a butterfly garden.

③ Swan Boats

MAP N4 ■ Public Garden ■ 617 522 1966 ■ Open mid-Apr–early Sep: usually 10am–5pm daily ■ Adm

If Boston were to have a mascot, it would likely sport white feathers and a graceful, arching neck. Round up the whole family and take to the Public Garden's lagoon on one of the city's iconic swan boats *(see p19)*.

④ Boston Duck Tours

MAP K6 ■ Prudential Center, New England Aquarium, and Museum of Science ■ 617 267 3825 ■ Open mid-Mar–Nov: 9am–dusk daily ■ Adm ■ www.bostonduck tours.com

Board a World War II-style amphibious vehicle that plies the Charles River as smoothly as it navigates Back Bay streets. This historic tour encompasses the entire peninsula and is conducted by informative and entertaining guides.

⑤ New England Aquarium

The aquarium *(see pp38–9)* goes to great lengths to keep kids entertained through a variety of interactive displays. Children are typically transfixed by penguins hopping and waddling in their rocky enclosure, and by the clowning antics of the harbor seals.

Loggerhead sea turtle at the New England Aquarium

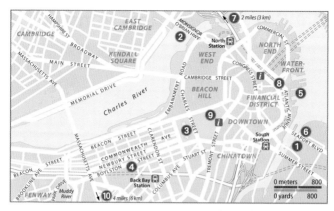

Kermit the Frog's statue, Frog Pond

6 Martin's Park
MAP R5 ▪ 64 Sleeper St

Named in honor of Martin Richard, the youngest victim of the 2013 Boston Marathon Bombing (see p43), this vibrant playground park is a welcome respite in the urban Seaport District.

7 Legoland® Discovery Center
MAP M4 ▪ 598 Assembly Row, Assembly Sq Mall, Somerville ▪ 617 702 5593 ▪ Open 10am–5pm daily ▪ Adm

A family entertainment center clubbed with a multiplex cinema, Legoland® is a prime attraction for children aged between 3 and 10. In addition to incredible tableaux made of Lego® bricks, the center has Lego® rides, a soft play center, and a bevy of Lego® characters. The highlight for many is the chance to build and test Lego® racers.

8 Greenway Carousel
MAP P1 ▪ Rose Kennedy Greenway ▪ Adm ▪ www.rose kennedygreenway.org

Set inside the Rose Kennedy Greenway, this charming seasonal carousel features hand-carved figures of 14 local animals, including a squirrel, turtle, cod, lobster, whale, three types of butterfly, and more. It is also accessible to individuals with specific requirements.

9 Frog Pond
MAP M4 ▪ Boston Common

As soon as temperatures dip below freezing, kids flock to the Frog Pond (see p18) for ice skating and hot chocolate at the adjacent hut. Boston's oft-oppressive summer days lure them back for splashing and fun beneath the central fountain.

10 Franklin Park Zoo
1 Franklin Park Rd, Dorchester ▪ 617 541 5466 ▪ Open 10am–5pm Mon–Fri, 10am–6pm Sat & Sun (Oct–Mar: 10am–4pm daily) ▪ Adm ▪ www.zoonewengland.com

Boston's urban zoo, dating back to 1913, houses over 200 species of animals. Its Tropical Forest section houses gorillas, leopards, and other exotic creatures. Bird's World showcases and provides a safe environment for dozens of species. The seasonal Franklin Farm lets kids get close to domestic farm animals.

🔟 Performing Arts Venues

Boston Pops Orchestra playing at the Symphony Hall

① Symphony Hall

Opened in 1900, Symphony Hall was designed by a Harvard physics professor Wallace Clement Sabine and is one of the world's most acoustically perfect concert venues. It is home to the internationally renowned Boston Symphony Orchestra and the Boston Pops (see p117). The BSO commissions new works, hosts world premieres, and frequently welcomes sought-after guest conductors and soloists.

② Boch Center – Wang Theatre

Capturing the gilded and marbled opulence of its muse, Versailles, the 3,500-seat Wang (see p107) is one of the city's most beautiful buildings. The Wang hosts touring productions from Broadway and London's West End as well as dance and opera productions by local companies.

③ Hatch Shell

MAP M3 ▪ The Esplanade ▪ 617 635 4505

Constructed in 1941, this shell (see p70) around a performance stage projects music across the Esplanade. Every Fourth of July (see p73) the Boston Pops Orchestra rings in Independence Day here. Free Friday Flicks brings firm family faves such as *The Wizard of Oz* and *Frozen* to the screen, while dance and music events occur almost nightly during summer.

④ Boston Center for the Arts

Home to three theater companies, four stages, and a gallery, the BCA (see p107) is the cornerstone of the South End arts scene. The artists who perform and exhibit here present some of the city's most provocative work. The Cyclorama, at the heart of the BCA, was built in 1884 to house a 360-degree painting of the Battle of Gettysburg.

The historic Somerville Theatre

⑤ Somerville Theatre

55 Davis Sq, Somerville ▪ 617 625 5700 ▪ www.somerville theatre.com

Extensive renovation has returned this Davis Square landmark to its original, ornate glory. When it isn't hosting some of the country's finest jazz, world music, and underground rock acts, the Somerville packs audiences in for feature films at low ticket prices.

6 New England Conservatory, Jordan Hall

MAP E6 ■ 30 Gainsborough St ■ 617 585 1260 ■ www.necmusic.edu

Dozens of local orchestral and choral ensembles call this hall home. Built at the turn of the 20th century and renowned for its intimacy and impressive acoustics, the hall hosts more than 450 free concerts a year.

7 Boston Opera House

MAP G4 ■ 539 Washington St ■ 617 259 3400 ■ www.bostonopera house.com

The Boston Opera House was one of the city's most ornate movie palaces when it opened in 1928. With a $54 million renovation in 2004, the theater was returned to its former glory, and today it presents a steady stream of mostly Broadway shows and is also the home of the Boston Ballet.

8 TD Garden

MAP G2 ■ 100 Legends Way ■ 617 624 1000 ■ www.tdgarden.com

Seating almost 20,000 and with over 3.5 million visitors a year, this arena is home to the NBA's Boston Celtics and the NHL's Boston Bruins, plus the Sports Museum of New England *(see p50)*. Aside from sporting events, it offers a full schedule of concerts, family entertainment, ice shows, and public events.

Berklee Performance Center

9 Berklee Performance Center

Berklee, the world's largest independent music college, boasts this premier venue *(see p89)*. The great acoustics ensure that some of the most highly distinguished jazz, folk, and world musicians play here. The student performances held here are usually free and among the best entertainment deals in town.

10 Sanders Theatre

MAP B1 ■ 45 Quincy St, Cambridge ■ 617 496 2222

Located in Harvard's splendid Memorial Hall *(see p20)*, this theater has hosted many luminaries over its 150-plus years. Great performers of the past century have graced its intimate stage, including mime artist Marcel Marceau. Henry Wadsworth Longfellow and Ralph Waldo Emerson *(see p45)* were among its early audiences.

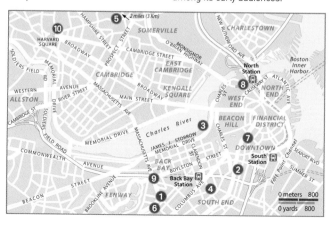

TOP 10 Dance and Live Music Venues

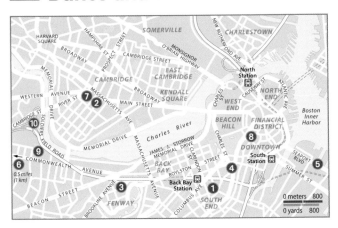

1 The Beehive

The nightly music mix at this venue *(see p111)* might sometimes veer toward cabaret or even burlesque, but local jazz musicians are the mainstay. Expect a well-dressed, mature crowd at least a decade past their schooldays, a convivial bar scene and excellent contemporary bistro fare. It all makes for a great night out.

2 The Middle East

The region's alternative rock scene can trace its genesis to this Central Square landmark. This influential venue has launched many careers, and seminal local bands like the Pixies, Mighty Mighty Bosstones, and Morphine have all played on The Middle East's three stages. Today, the club *(see p128)* continues the tradition, genuinely embracing musicians operating just under the mainstream radar.

3 House of Blues

The House of Blues chain *(see p120)* was born across the river in Cambridge, before moving to its current location behind Fenway Park in 2003. Since then, the House of Blues has been an integral part of the student-friendly Lansdowne Street nightlife scene, playing live music to 2,400 people each night. The program celebrates American music: gospel, jazz, R&B, roots-based rock 'n' roll, and, of course, blues.

Decor at the House of Blues

4 Royale

Housed in an ornate, bi-level theater, the Royale *(see p111)* can accommodate more dancers than any other Boston club. Top 40, 1980s, Latin, and house music are pumped

Lauryn Hill performing at Royale

through the powerful sound system, while a mixed crowd lounges around on cushy banquettes or throngs the mammoth dance floor.

5 Leader Bank Pavilion
MAP H4 ■ 290 Northern Ave ■ 617 728 1600 ■ Adm

This circular 1-acre (0.4 ha) outdoor amphitheater, originally known as Harbor Lights, is one of Boston's prime summer concert venues. It has the capacity to seat more than 5,000 spectators beneath a grand tent that shields them from inclement weather. Cool harbor breezes and state-of-the-art lighting and sound systems enhance the experience.

6 Brighton Music Hall
MAP A4 ■ 158 Brighton Ave ■ 617 779 0140 ■ Adm

Set in the heart of Allston, Brighton Music Hall primarily caters to college and university students. The 400-capacity concert hall hosts up-and-coming national and local rock, pop, alternative, and indie rock bands as well as stand-up comedy shows.

7 Havana Club
MAP C2 ■ 288 Green St, Cambridge ■ 617 312 5550 (text message only) ■ Adm

Located in the heart of Central Square, this dance club holds five bachata and salsa parties a week (Monday, Tuesday and Thursday to Saturday nights)

with lessons available before the party starts. Singles are always welcome.

8 Orpheum Theatre
MAP G4 ■ 1 Hamilton Pl ■ 617 482 0106 ■ Adm

Boston's oldest music venue, the Orpheum dates from 1852. After serving as a vaudeville house and a movie theater, it has now become a beloved venue for touring rock bands and comedy concerts.

9 Paradise Rock Club
MAP C5 ■ 967 Commonwealth Ave ■ 617 562 8800 ■ Adm

Although no longer in its original Downtown location, the Paradise is the oldest name in Boston rock venues. Icons from the 1970s and 1980s such as Van Halen, the Police, and Blondie first put the club on the map. Today, the Paradise remains true to its rock 'n' roll roots, welcoming nationally recognized acts that favor volume levels north of ten.

Performers at Scullers Jazz Club

10 Scullers Jazz Club
MAP C4 ■ 400 Soldiers Field Rd ■ 866 777 8932 ■ Closed Sun ■ Adm

Enthusiastic champion of Latin jazz and emerging artists (Norah Jones and Diana Krall started here), Scullers is also a well-known venue for internationally established musicians. It's a great place to enjoy a drink and an evening of smooth jazz by some of the best performers in the business.

LGBTQ+ Venues

Classy interior of Club Café

① Club Café
MAP M6 ▪ 209 Columbus Ave
This multifunctional South End space combines cabaret, a piano bar, a dance club and an American bistro, drawing in a young crowd each night. Check out the video lounge, order a drink from the mirrored bar or the sleek cocktail lounge, or opt to chow down on the famous Sunday brunch. The restaurant gives classic continental fare an inspired twist.

② Midway Café
3496 Washington St, Jamaica Plain ▪ Adm
Having offered its stage to rockabilly, punk, swing, reggae, and hip-hop acts since 1987, the Midway Café is partially responsible for Jamaica Plain's (see p132) youth-driven renaissance. The club's Thursday Queeraoke Night is one of the most popular lesbian club night events in town, while other nights of the week bring in edgy music lovers from all over the city.

③ dbar
This inviting Dorchester spot (see p134), with its warm wood and brass interior, has a dual personality: trendy, full-service neighborhood bistro by day, popular gay dance club at night. Love Broadway musicals? "Show Tunes Tuesdays" are a wildly popular sing-along that can get a bit rowdy late in the evening.

④ Diesel Café
257 Elm St, Somerville
This hipster-filled coffee shop, in the heart of Somerville's bustling Davis Square, is a favorite hangout among the area's LGBTQ+ couples. Here, they guzzle gourmet coffee, sip inventive teas, and snack on tasty treats, while soaking up the relaxed vibe and chatting the afternoon away.

⑤ Machine
MAP E5 ▪ 1254 Boylston St ▪ Adm
A facelift saw Machine absorb the notorious Ramrod hook-up bar that used to be in the same building. It is now a two-story nightclub catering to the LGBTQ+ community and its allies with themed nights, including drag shows, and karaoke; DJ-led dance nights featuring the best dance music of the 1980s, 1990s, and 2000s help round out the offerings. As a result, the dance floor is packed most nights, but particularly so on weekends. Join the go-go dancers and bust a move.

Popular nightclub Machine

⑥ Guerilla Queer Bar
www.thewelcomingcommittee. com/boston#boston-takeovers
This is not a place, but a viral event. On the first Friday of each month scores, and sometimes hundreds, of LGBTQ+ partygoers descend on a chosen bar or nightclub. The result is fun and

uplifting for everyone – so much so that it is becoming a nationwide phenomenon. Check the website for the forthcoming venue.

7 The Alley Bar
MAP P3 ■ 275 Washington St
■ 617 263 1449

Hosting activities like karaoke and pool tournaments, The Alley has a mellow, sociable vibe. There is an upstairs/downstairs set-up which gives the casual drinkers a space away from the theme-night partiers. The bar's menu consists of comfort American food including chicken wings and a range of draft and bottled beers.

8 Cathedral Station
MAP N6 ■ 1222 Washington St ■ 617 868 6060

Located in the South End near Holy Cross Cathedral, this casual and spacious neighborhood sports bar is geared towards an LGBTQ+ clientele, but everyone is welcome. This venue is also the de facto home of several LGBTQ+ sports leagues.

9 Jacque's Cabaret
One of the oldest names on the Boston gay club scene, and discreetly tucked away behind the Theater District, Jacque's *(see p111)* has been welcoming queer rock bands and drag queens, and their adoring fans for many decades.

Jacque's Cabaret

It is a lively option every night of the week, with garage rock and beer fueling the pool-playing crowd.

10 Boston Eagle
MAP F6 ■ 520 Tremont St

A doorway-mounted wooden eagle has welcomed everyone to this subterranean South End bar for years. Frequented by the LGBTQ+ community, the Boston Eagle is regarded as an institution. The dimly lit bar area is roomy and comfortable; in the back, a mirrored wall captures pool sharks and pinball wizards at work.

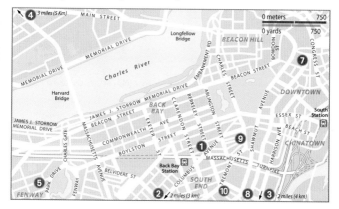

🔟 **Bars**

① Drink
MAP R5 ▪ 348 Congress St
▪ 617 695 1806

This trendy subterranean bar in the Fort Point district wins praise for its impressive lineup of classic and classically inspired cocktails. Order the house signature drink – the Fort Point version of the Manhattan – or ask the knowledgeable bartenders to create a unique drink based on your taste and preferences.

② Haley.Henry Wine Bar
A local favorite, Haley.Henry is a small, stylish wine bar *(see p104)* located in the heart of Downtown Crossing. Known for its thoughtfully curated wine list, which is available by the glass as well as by the half-bottle, the bar also serves beer. The menu features cheese and charcuterie boards, crudo, and imported varieties of tinned fish.

③ Oak Long Bar & Kitchen
The Copley Plaza hotel bar *(see p92)* serves a full roster of craft cocktails and a farm-to-table seasonal dining menu. In summer, drinks and meals can be enjoyed on the outdoor patio, which appropriately enough overlooks the twice-weekly farmers' market.

④ Delux Café
You will be reluctant to let the secret out about this spot. The intimate Delux Café *(see p111)*, located in South End, attracts a refreshing mix of professionals, bike messengers, and members of the LGBTQ+ community. The bar features a kitschy motif of Elvis Presley, extensive on-tap beers, and a constant broadcast of the Cartoon Network.

⑤ Street Bar
Originally the cigar lounge of Boston's first luxury hotel, the Street Bar *(see p92)* is a great place for sipping a dram of Scotch by a fireplace or enjoying craft cocktails that are bound to become classics in their own right.

⑥ Tavern in the Square
MAP P1 ▪ 120 Beverly St
▪ 617 263 0404

Located across the street from the TD Garden, this is the go-to sports bar for Celtics and Bruins fans when they can't get tickets to a game. Fifty beers on tap are complemented by a good pub-grub menu. The Sunday brunch is both popular and peculiar, featuring the likes of Nutella French toast and a doughnut burger.

Plush furnishings and tasteful decor of Oak Long Bar & Kitchen

Jazz musicians at Regattabar

7 Regattabar
The giants of jazz often stop at this nautical-themed lounge (see p128) in Cambridge's Charles Hotel. Drinks may not be extraordinary but the talent is; past visitors have included McCoy Tyner, Ron Carter, and local favorite the Charlie Kolhase Quintet. Shows sell out quickly so buy tickets in advance.

8 Backbar
During the extension of the green MBTA line to Union Square, Backbar (see p128) was an oasis amid the construction work. With its entrance hidden behind several restaurants, this cocktail bar still has a speakeasy vibe and draws cocktail aficionados to Somerville to try its innovative concoctions.

9 City Winery
Located close to TD Garden, this relaxed wine bar and restaurant (see p85) has a well-designed performance space that hosts live music concerts as well as stand-up comedy shows. There's also a winery on site that conducts tours and tastings, and is a perfect place to sample different wines on tap.

10 Alibi
Set in the former drunk tank of the Charles Street Jail (now the posh Liberty Hotel), Alibi (see p85) retains the bluestone floors and vestiges of the cell walls to form little nooks to lounge in while you enjoy your drinks. If the weather permits, opt to have a drink on the patio at sundown. There's also an upscale Italian restaurant on site.

TOP 10 LOCALLY BREWED BEERS

1 Awake, Night Shift
Porter aged with coffee picks you up and puts you down.

2 Harpoon IPA, Harpoon
Ranked among the top domestic and imported India pale ales by *Beer Connoisseur Magazine*.

3 Casual Gods, Cambridge Brewing Company
A superb barrel-fermented golden wild ale with a fruity yeast character.

4 Congress Street IPA, Trillium
Tropical fruit notes and citrusy hops dominate this flagship IPA at Trillium.

5 617 Hazy IPA, Lord Hobo
Named after the Boston telephone area code, this beer packs a punch at 6.17 per cent alcohol by volume.

6 Boston Lager, Samuel Adams
The beer that put Sam back on the brewing map after a 200-year hiatus.

7 Metric Systems, Lamplighter
Only at Cambridge taproom, this lemon-tangy Gose wheat beer is a brewery signature.

8 Cherry Wheat Ale, Samuel Adams
Like a hybrid between champagne and cherry soda, this brew is available at most liquor stores.

9 UFO Hefeweizen, Harpoon
Try this unfiltered, Belgian-style brew, with fruity undertones.

10 Octoberfest, Samuel Adams
Sam's finest – available only during the autumn – with deep amber coloring and a warm, spicy smoothness.

Samuel Adams Octoberfest mugs

☒☒ Restaurants

① Oleana

Located on a charming street outside Cambridge's busy Kendall Square, Oleana *(see p129)* introduces diners to fragrant Turkish and Middle Eastern flavors and spice-laden dishes made from local and seasonal produce. The restaurant is both revelatory and pleasing to a wide range of palates – offering hearty lamb as well as *mezze*. Sit outside on the patio or inside by the woodstove.

Elegant seating at Oleana

② Uni

Local culinary titan Ken Oringer and chef-partner Tony Messina operate this lively, upscale *izakaya (see p93)* in the ground level of Back Bay's Eliot Hotel. Small plates of global street food dot the menu, along with fresh takes on *makimoni*, *nigiri*, and *sashimi*. Cult ramen meals are served late on weekend nights.

Uni's tuna sashimi

③ Pammy's

Referred to as a "New American *trattoria*" by the owners, Pammy's *(see p129)* is a cozy and welcoming restaurant that makes diners feel like house guests. Located between Harvard and Central Square in Cambridge, this spot has a distinctive American take on Italian cuisine. The limited menu features innovative dishes, such as mussels with squid ink aranchini and lime-leaf aioli, as well as local striped bass with Italian garbanzo beans, strawberries, and reduced grape must.

④ Grill 23 & Bar

Easily Boston's finest steakhouse, Grill 23 *(see p93)* features one of the city's best wine lists and a number of delicious alternatives to seared slabs of perfect beef. Swordfish, sea bass, salmon, and lobster satisfy the pescatarians. Sides include lobster mac and cheese with smoked Gouda, and fries with a house harissa ketchup.

⑤ Trade

A fine-dining anchor to the Greenway Park, the Trade *(see p99)* links Downtown and the waterfront. Set in the Atlantic Wharf building, it makes use of Mediterranean flavors while remaining true to its New England roots. Both ends of that historic trade route shine in dishes such as braised short rib with Jerusalem artichoke, olives, and orange. The restaurant is popular for its light lunches, which feature freshly made sandwiches and salads.

⑥ Toro

Chef-owners Ken Oringer and Jamie Bissonnette team up for one of the city's hardest-to-get-into restaurants *(see p113)*. This South End hot spot serves Barcelona-inspired hot and cold small plates, which are designed to be enjoyed tapas-style. The unmissable order? A charcuterie board. Add a creative cocktail program and an eclectic wine list, and it's no wonder that Toro is as popular at cocktail hour as it is at dinner.

Menton's exquisite cuisine

7 Menton

Superchef Barbara Lynch's elegant Fort Point dining room (see p99) regularly receives national-level rave reviews. Diners can choose from one of two tasting menus, with offerings such as lobster and chamomile with fava, hazelnut, and Meyer lemon; or tart of foie gras enhanced with wild ramps, beetroot, and spring onion. It is requested that all diners at a table choose the same menu.

8 Craigie On Main

Award-winning chef Tony Maws, acclaimed for his French-inspired nose-to-tail approach to fine dining, presides over a bustling open kitchen facing the dining area, filled with a mix of foodies on a pilgrimage and couples celebrating an occasion. The menu at Craigie On Main (see p129) changes daily, based on the locally sourced organic ingredients at the market that morning. Head to the bar for the wildly popular gourmet burger, served with big, chunky fries, and great cocktails.

9 No. 9 Park

Chef Barbara Lynch opened this intimate restaurant as her first fine-dining establishment in 1998. Today, No. 9 Park (see p105) remains the flagship showcase of her stylish approach to Mediterranean cuisine that borrows a little from France, a little from Italy, and a lot from her imagination. Great sommeliers help explain the vast and interesting wine list.

10 Harvest

Since the 1970s, this restaurant (see p129) has been a leader in setting the direction of American cuisine. Chef Nick Deutmayer brings a Mediterranean palate to New England cuisine, pairing lobster with favas and nasturtium blossoms or roasting pork with local fennel, garlic, and stone fruits. The outdoor garden terrace is lovely.

Bar at Harvest

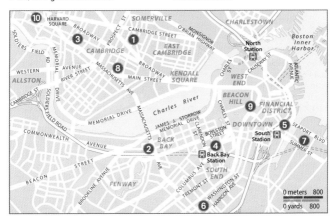

🔟 Spots for Seafood

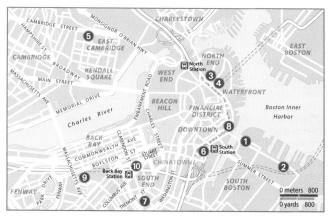

1 James Hook & Co.

MAP H5 ■ 15 Northern Ave ■ 617 423 5500 ■ Closed evenings ■ $

A family-owned business located right on Fort Point Channel, Hook is primarily a broker that supplies lobster to restaurants throughout the US. However, they also cook lobster, clams, crab, and some fin fish on the spot. Take your order, sit on the sea wall, and chow down. Many visitors find it the best place to eat good, reasonably priced seafood.

2 Legal Harborside

The Seaport flagship (see p99) of the Legal Sea Foods chain has aced dockside dining. You'll find a no-frills, casual dining room, oyster bar, and a traditional fish market on level one; there's fine dining featuring beautifully prepared fish on level two; while level three offers a four-season rooftop lounge and bar, with a retractable glass roof and walls, serving ocean-fresh sushi and cocktails. All three spaces come with a stunning harbor view.

Dish at Legal Harborside

3 Neptune Oyster

Exceptionally fresh choices from the raw bar vie for attention with dishes from the expertly prepared dinner menu. Choose an old favorite, such as clam chowder, or a more daring dish like Spanish octopus with hazelnut romesco. The simple dining room of this restaurant (see p99) ensures that the food is the focus of attention. Reservations are not accepted so arrive early and be prepared to wait for a table – it's worth it.

4 Mare Oyster Bar

Located in Boston's historic North End, Mare (see p99) specializes in Italian coastal cuisine. Begin with the raw bar or a trio of crudos, then savor a classic seafood pasta dish or grilled fish – or indulge yourself with a decadent lobster roll on brioche, along with a plate of fries. The spicy fish gnocchi is a must try. A few meat dishes are also available. To accompany your meal, enjoy a cocktail or glass of wine from their enticing drinks menu.

5 Courthouse Seafood

A stalwart in its Portuguese neighborhood since 1912, the Courthouse *(see p129)* offers dishes prepared with the fresh catch of the day. The restaurant's menu brims with sautéed or fried squid, lightly breaded and deep-fried smelt, and broiled haddock or salmon. During July to September, try the intensely flavored bluefish.

6 O Ya

Combining Japanese tradition and American invention, this elegant restaurant *(see p105)* proves that good things come in small packages. Offering both sweet and savoury dishes, half the menu is sushi and *sashimi*, and the other half is made up of meat and vegetarian options. With six chefs at work, each bite-sized portion is exquisitely executed. Ask for the *omakase* (tasting) menu and let the head chef Tim Cushman wow you with a culinary tour de force.

The bar at B&G Oysters

7 B&G Oysters

This brightly lit underground seafood spot *(see p113)* is both oyster bar – there are a dozen varieties ready to be shucked at any moment – and seafood bistro.

8 Barking Crab

This colorful fish shack *(see p99)* is most congenial in the summer, when diners sit outdoors at picnic tables, but there's also indoor seating with a cozy wood-burner for chillier days. Most of the local fish – cod, haddock, tuna, halibut, clams,

Barking Crab fish shack

and crab – are so fresh that they need only the simplest preparation. There is also a good selection of wines and craft beers on offer.

9 Summer Shack

Boston celebrity chef Jasper White literally wrote the book on lobster, but he's just as adept with wood-grilled fresh fish and delicate fried shellfish. A fabulous raw bar and colorful summer fish-shack atmosphere match well with the extensive beer list. Re-creating the ambience of a beachside seafood shack in the city, this spot *(see p93)* is a great place to bring kids.

10 Banks Fish House

The seafood sister to steak-lovers' Grill 23 *(see p62)*, Banks Fish House *(see p93)* has a beautiful dining space, with three fireplaces, two bars, and an open kitchen, split across two levels. On any given day, the menu will feature oysters from a half dozen New England harbors and the latest local seasonal catch. Dine casually on chowder, pizza, or fish tacos at the bar or reserve a table to indulge in a seafood feast, complemented by a dazzling wine list.

The Fisherman's Platter at Banks

For a key to restaurant price ranges see p85

🔟 Cafés

Comfortable split-level interior of Thinking Cup

1 Thinking Cup
MAP G4 ■ 165 Tremont St

A cozy place to socialize on Boston Common, Thinking Cup serves teas and Stumptown-roasted coffee. Knowledgeable baristas offer assistance with your choice of espresso drinks or pour-overs. The menu also includes tempting pastries and sandwiches.

2 Pavement Coffee
MAP J6 ■ 1096 Boylston St

This local roaster offers a range of different coffee roasts in every-thing from pour-overs to espresso. The freshly made bagels are also popular with students of the nearby Berklee College.

3 Caffè Vittoria
MAP Q1 ■ 296 Hanover St

The jukebox at the largest of North End's Italian cafés is heavily loaded with songs recorded by Frank Sinatra, Tony Bennett, and Al Martino. The menu is long on short coffees and short drinks, including at least seven varieties of grappa, as well as Italian ices. The café accepts cash only.

4 Mike's Pastry

Legendary for its 20 or so flavors of fresh *cannolis*, Mike's Pastry (*see p98*) is one of Boston's most loved bakeries. Here is a café where all sorts of baked goodies are available, including cupcakes, biscotti, brownies, cakes, pies, cookies, and specialty items – along with gourmet brews. The lines outside Mike's can be long, especially on weekends, but they do tend to move quickly.

5 Sonsie
MAP J6 ■ 327 Newbury St

Although continental breakfast is served, Sonsie doesn't really get going until lunchtime. By dusk, it is full of folks who just stopped in for a post-work drink and ended up making an evening of it. The food – pizza, pasta, and fusion-tinged entrées – deserves more attention than most café-goers give it.

6 Tatte Bakery & Café
MAP B1 ■ 1288 Massachusetts Ave, Cambridge

Featuring an artfully curated menu by master pastry chef Tzurit Or, Tatte's Harvard Square branch has a strik-ing decor with an open kitchen and bakery on the first floor, and a coffee bar on the second floor. Hipsters, Harvard staff and students, and locals flock here to get their fix of caffeine and heavenly pastries, tarts, cookies, as well as quiches.

7 1369 Coffee House

A community-based café, 1369 Coffee House has a definite neighborly atmosphere. The original Inman Square branch (*see p127*) has a more interesting cross section of characters but the Central Square outpost has sidewalk seating. Both branches serve caffeine drinks, sweets, and sandwiches at lunch.

8 Dado Tea
This eco-friendly shop serves a choice of blends, alongside organic wraps, sandwiches, and salads as well as white, black, and green teas. Dado Tea (see p127) offers a selection of gluten-free and vegan options too. Coffee-lovers are accommodated, but tea rules here.

9 Phinista Cafe
MAP E4 ▪ 96 Peterborough St
This French–Vietnamese café brews *phin* coffee in all its dizzying array of variations. Think coffee mixed with egg yolk and condensed milk, and a vegan latte made with condensed coconut milk. The house favorite tea is *oolong*, often served with steamed milk. Star anise and cloves flavor the popular "Milk n' Thai" tea.

10 Sorelle Bakery & Cafe
MAP H4 ▪ 100 Northern Ave
The Seaport branch of this local coffee and sweets emporium serves all of your regular coffee options and has a nice selection of freshly brewed teas as well. Local early risers flock here each morning for a frittata sandwich with ciabatta bread or a bowl of steel-cut oatmeal; the cranberry muffins are a hit, too.

Breakfast at Sorelle Bakery & Cafe

TOP 10 SPOTS TO BREAK YOUR DIET

L. A. Burdick Chocolatiers

1 L. A. Burdick Chocolatiers
MAP B1 ▪ 52D Brattle St, Cambridge
Burdick's rich hot chocolate is one of Boston's most popular winter treats.

2 Swissbäkers
MAP B2 ▪ 168 Western Ave
This modern bakery serves pretzels, baguettes, sandwiches, and cookies.

3 Union Square Donuts
20 Bow St, Somerville
Classic donut flavors are supplemented with surprising seasonal specialties.

4 La Sultana Bakery
40 Maverick Sq, East Boston
Empanadas and other Columbian delicacies are served at this bakery.

5 Flour Bakery & Café
MAP F6; 1595 Washington St ▪ MAP R5; 12 Farnsworth St
This spot excels at breakfast pastries, lunchtime sandwiches, and cookies.

6 Beacon Hill Chocolates
MAP F3 ▪ 91 Charles St
Sweet shop selling artisan chocolates from around the globe.

7 Eldo Cake House
MAP P4 ▪ 36 Harrison Ave
Eldo Cake House serves Western-style iced cakes and Chinese treats.

8 Lizzy's Ice Cream
MAP B1 ▪ 29 Church St, Cambridge
The ice cream offered here has toppings such as chopped candy bars.

9 Sofra Bakery & Cafe
1 Belmont St, Cambridge
Try the baklava or a *dukkah* (an Egyptian condiment) macaroon at this bakery.

10 Christina's Homemade Ice Cream
MAP D2 ▪ 1255 Cambridge St, Cambridge
Exciting flavors of ice cream are served with fresh fruits and exotic spices.

🔟 Essential Shopping Experiences

1 Boston Public Market
MAP Q2 ■ 100 Hanover St

Modern public market features around 40 farmers, fishers, and other small food producers in bright setting. The many vendors of prepared food make it a good breakfast or lunch option. A demo kitchen hosts various activities.

2 Garment District
MAP D2 ■ 200 Broadway, Cambridge

The vintage clothing and bargain-priced trends of the Garment District are every Boston hipster's retort to fashion. Fancy-dress costumes are found on the first floor, but you can also find retro goods, office wear, and even clothing sold by the pound.

3 Faneuil Hall Marketplace

With its millions of visitors each year, Faneuil Hall Marketplace *(see p101)* would not be found on any best-kept secret list. Its central location, rich colonial history, and plethora of food stalls in Quincy Market mean that it offers a unique retail experience. Shoppers can choose from name-brand stores such as UNIQLO or the more unusual offerings from New England artisans.

Georgian-style facade of Faneuil Hall

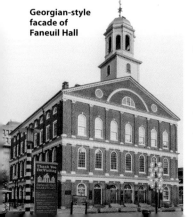

4 Copley Place
MAP L6 ■ 100 Huntington Ave

This was among the country's first upscale urban shopping malls. It counts high-end stores such as Louis Vuitton, Tiffany, Neiman Marcus, and Coach as its tenants. Footwear addicts are fond of Stuart Weitzman and Jimmy Choo boutiques.

Red Sox merchandise

5 Red Sox Team Store
MAP D5 ■ 19 Jersey St

With World Series titles dating back to 1903 and the oldest ballpark in professional baseball, the Boston Red Sox engender a fan loyalty matched by few other teams. This memorabilia shop, across the street from Fenway Park *(see p117)*, sells every permutation of hat, jersey, and T-shirt imaginable, as well as signed bats, balls, and gloves, and baseball cards for hardcore collectors.

6 Newbury Street

Try as it might, Back Bay's most famous street cannot escape its regional reputation as the city's Beverly Hills' Rodeo Drive. True, both offer stupendous people-watching, sophisticated shopping, chic dining, and prestigious galleries. Yet, with its 19th-century charm and convenient subway stops, Newbury Street *(see pp24–5)* outclasses its built-yesterday Left Coast counterpart by far.

Shelves brimming with books at the Harvard Coop bookstore

7 Harvard Square Bookstores
MAP B1

Harvard Square's bookstores are some of the country's most distinguished. The Harvard Coop *(1400 Massachusetts Ave)* carries 170,000-plus titles, while rival Harvard Book Store *(1256 Massachusetts Ave)* stocks countless new and used books and hosts readings. Nearby Grolier Poetry Bookshop *(6 Plympton St)* is verse central, while Raven Used Books *(23 Church St)* stocks 15,000 academic and literary titles.

8 Charles Street
MAP M3

This charming street is studded with antiques dealers *(see p84)*, specialty grocers, and modern houseware boutiques. After dark, wrought-iron lamps illuminate the sidewalks and sleek bistros buzz with excitement.

9 Artists' Open Studios
www.boston.gov/depart ments/arts-and-culture

Boston's visual artists open their studios, which are mostly found in converted warehouses, to the public on selected spring and fall weekends. One of the most popular is the South End Open Studio event. Start at the Boston Center for the Arts *(see p54)*, where you can pick up a map, before exploring the many studios nearby.

10 SoWa Open Market
MAP G6 ■ 500 Harrison Ave

Expect a wide range of clothing, jewelry, and art at Boston's art and indie design market, held every Sunday from May to October in the South End. Hungry? Check out fresh local produce at the farmers' market or take your pick from the many food trucks.

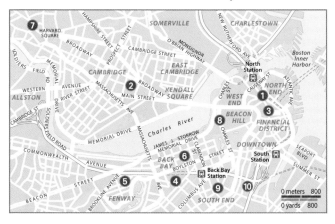

Boston for Free

USS *Constitution* or "Old Ironsides"

1 Charlestown Navy Yard

Home to the Revolutionary War-era frigate USS *Constitution*, the Charlestown Navy Yard *(see pp36–7)* is one of the oldest shipbuilding facilities in the country. Also here is the 1943 destroyer USS *Cassin Young*. Both admission to the yard and the ranger-led tours of the ships are free.

2 Hatch Shell

Free family movie nights are held on Fridays from late June through August at the Hatch Shell *(see p54)*, located on the banks of the Charles River. This spot also hosts free concerts throughout the summer, including Boston Pops' Fourth of July concert.

3 Mount Auburn Cemetery

580 Mt Auburn St, Cambridge ■ 617 547 7105 ■ www.mount auburn.org

A great place to take a walk in the city is Mount Auburn Cemetery, which serves as a park, botanical garden and arboretum, as well as the final resting place of luminaries ranging from poet Henry Wadsworth Longfellow to inventor Buckminster Fuller. The beautiful grounds feature 3 miles (5 km) of walking trails and quiet roadways.

4 Black Heritage Trail

In the 19th century, Boston's thriving Black community was a driving force in the fight to end slavery and, in the 20th century, they strove to achieve equality. A free National Park Service tour of the Black Heritage Trail *(see p82)* visits a diverse range of historic homes, schools, and businesses that tell the story of Boston's early African American citizens. Included are visits to the first public school for Black people in America and the 1806 African Meeting House.

5 Freedom Trail

Walking the self-guided Freedom Trail *(see pp12–13)* is one of the most popular activities for visitors in Boston. Touring the trail is free, as are entering all but 4 of the 16 sites and attractions along the way. Allow at least half a day for this stroll through history.

Freedom Trail Town Crier

6 Harvard Square

MAP C2 ■ www.harvard square.com

One of Boston's liveliest public spaces is also a great place for people-watching. There are always buskers performing, and it hosts a regular schedule of events including outdoor musical and theater performances. In September, thousands of locals come to take part in the free, one-night RiverSing to celebrate the fall equinox.

People gathered in Harvard Square

7 Shakespeare on Boston Common

MAP N2 ▪ 617 426 0863 ▪ www.commshakes.org

The Commonwealth Shakespeare Company performs one of the Bard's plays free-of-charge on Boston Common each July and August. Perfomances may be preceded by free musical concerts.

8 Boston HarborWalk

www.bostonharbornow.org

Connecting public parks, historic sites, as well as points of interest from East Boston to Dorchester, HarborWalk is an ideal place for cycling or walking. When completed it will stretch 43 miles (69 km).

Stretch of Boston HarborWalk

9 Fort Independence

Fort Independence on Castle Island (see p46), at the entrance to Boston's inner harbor, was a cutting-edge military defense system when it was begun in 1834. Free tours are available in summer. Be sure to stop at Sullivan's legendary hot-dog stand, which is found nearby.

10 Free Guided Tours

There are many free guided tours available around Boston. Three of the most popular take in the Freedom Trail (see pp12–13), Faneuil Hall (see p101), and the Boston Public Library (see p87). Other options include tours of Harvard Yard (see pp20–21) and the Massachusetts State House (see p15).

TOP 10 BUDGET TIPS

BosTix ticket booth

1 Bargain Tickets
www.artsboston.org
BosTix kiosks sell discounted tickets to many events on performance day.

2 CityPass
www.citypass.com
A CityPass ($64) gives discounted access to four top sights.

3 Go Boston Card
www.gocity.com
Save up to 55 per cent on entry to a wide range of sights with this card.

4 Public Transit Passes
MBTA passes allow unlimited travel on subways, buses, and ferries (see p138).

5 Museum Admission
Some museums, such as the Museum of Fine Arts, offer free or discounted admission at certain times.

6 Special Discounts
Student and senior citizen discounts are often available with identification.

7 College Galleries
College and university art galleries offer some of the city's most provocative exhibitions, often with free admission.

8 Boston Symphony Savings
Reduced-price tickets for people under age 40 and limited $10 rush seats are available at Symphony Hall (see p54).

9 Theater Deals
www.huntingtontheatre.org
The Huntington Theatre has $30 tickets for under-35s; as well as a limited number of $25 tickets for all ages at every performance.

10 Music Schools
Berklee Performance Center (see p55) offers low-cost and free concerts. The New England Conservatory holds free performances at Jordan Hall (see p55).

Festivals and Events

Dancers celebrating the Chinese New Year

Chinese New Year
Jan/Feb

Chinatown (see pp106–113) buzzes with the pageantry of the Chinese New Year. Streets are transformed into patchworks of color, while side-walk vendors peddle steamed buns, soups, and other Chinese delights. Don't miss the annual parade, held the Saturday following the Lunar New Year.

Boston Flower and Garden Show
Mid-Mar ■ www.bostonflower show.com

Over 150,000 visitors descend on this week-long indoor exhibition, hosted at the Seaport World Trade Center, to forget their winter blues and enjoy the spectacular display of bright blooms and fragrant aromas.

St. Patrick's Day
Mid-Mar

Boston's immense Irish American population explains why few, if any, American cities can match its Irish pride. Come Paddy's Day, pubs host live Irish bands and increasingly raucous crowds as the Guinness and the Shamrock-green ale flow freely. The weekend South Boston Parade, with its famous drum corps, starts off from Broadway "T" station.

④ Dine Out Boston
Mar & Aug ■ www. bostonusa.com/dine-out-boston

For two weeks in March and August, about 100 restaurants in Boston, Cambridge, and neighboring suburbs offer bargain, fixed-price lunch and dinner menus. Locals look forward to, and make the most of, the oppor-tunity to sample new restaurants, so it is wise to make reservations.

⑤ Lilac Sunday
2nd Sun in May ■ www. arboretum.harvard.edu

While the Arnold Arboretum (see p131) includes 4,463 species of flora, one plant deserves particular celebration. When its 400 lilac plants are at their fragrant, color-washed peak, garden enthusiasts arrive in droves for picnics, music, and walking tours of the lilac collections.

Boston Calling
Late May ■ www.boston calling.com

National headliners and new, up-and-coming acts perform live, with non-stop music for three days in late May at the Harvard Athletic Complex, to sell-out crowds. It's a family-friendly festival, with three stages and a good variety of high-energy performers and musical styles. In recent years, Boston Calling has featured the likes of Beck, the Pixies, Kendrick Lamar, Lorde, and the Alabama Shakes.

Cambridge Arts River Festival
Early Jun ■ www.cambridgema. gov/arts/Programs/riverfestival

On a Saturday in early June, the banks of the Charles River in

Cambridge host a celebration of the city's lively and diverse population. Musicians and dancers perform and artists sell their wares. Food vendors serve a variety of cuisines.

Fourth of July
Jul 4

Given Boston's crucial role in securing independence for the original 13 colonies, Independence Day holds a certain importance here. With parties, barbecues, a concert, and fireworks display over the Charles River banks, the city throws a spectacular birthday party.

Boston's Fourth of July fireworks

Feast of St. Anthony
Last weekend in Aug

The Feast of St. Anthony caps an entire summer of feast holidays in the North End (see pp94–9). From noon through well into the night, Hanover Street bulges with revelers, a procession, and food vendors giving a vibrant display of the area's Italian spirit.

First Night
Dec 31

Despite the possibility of staggeringly cold weather, the New Year's Eve festivities remain among the most highly anticipated events of Boston's year. Free and open to all, the events are usually held around Copley Square and Back Bay. They include a parade, beautifully lit ice sculptures, light displays, and family-friendly fireworks at 7pm on the Common.

TOP 10 SPORTS TRADITIONS AND TEAMS

Boston Celtics in action

1 New Year's Day Swim
Jan 1
The "L Street Brownies" swimming club takes a dip in Boston Harbor.

2 Beanpot Hockey Tournament
1st & 2nd Mon in Feb ▪ 617 624 1000
Boston's top collegiate hockey teams compete with each other.

3 New England Revolution
Mar–Nov ▪ 800 543 1776
The local entry in the annual Major League Soccer at Gillette Stadium.

4 Boston Red Sox
Apr–Oct ▪ 617 267 1700
The most heated rivalry in US sports flares up every time the Yanks visit Fenway Park (see p117).

5 Boston Marathon
3rd Mon in Apr ▪ 617 236 1652
The country's oldest marathon attracts international participants.

6 New England Patriots
Sep–Feb ▪ 800 543 1776
Gillette Stadium is the home of the Patriots, six-time Super Bowl champs.

7 Boston Bruins
Oct–Jun ▪ 617 624 1000
Crowds cheer this ice hockey team at the TD Garden.

8 Boston Celtics
Oct–Jun ▪ 617 624 1000
The Celts keep basketball playoff dreams alive at the TD Garden.

9 Head of the Charles Regatta
3rd Sat & Sun in Oct ▪ 617 868 6200
Rowing crews race down the Charles while the banks teem with onlookers.

10 Harvard vs Yale
Nov ▪ 617 495 3454
These Ivy League football teams butt helmets every even-numbered year.

TOP 10 Day Trips: Historic New England

1 Lexington
Massachusetts ■ **Route 2**
■ **Visitor information:** 1875 Massachusetts Ave; 1 781 862 1450 ■ www.lexingtonchamber.org

Lexington Green marks the first encounter of invading British soldiers with organized resistance from American troops. This military band took shelter in Buckman Tavern the night before the battle.

Minuteman statue, Lexington Green

2 Concord
Massachusetts ■ **Route 2**
■ **Visitor information:** 58 Main St; 1 978 318 3061 ■ www.concordma.gov

Rebels put the Redcoats to rout at North Bridge, Concord's main revolutionary battle site. The town was also the hub of American literature in the mid-19th century, and visitors can tour the homes of authors Ralph Waldo Emerson, Nathaniel Hawthorne, and Louisa May Alcott. Henry David Thoreau's woodland haunts at Walden Pond now feature hiking trails and a swimming beach.

3 New Bedford
Massachusetts ■ **Routes I-95 & I-195** ■ **Visitor information:** 33 William St; 1 508 996 4095 ■ www.nps.gov/nebe

During the 19th century, local whaling vessels hunted the oceans of the world, enriching the port of New Bedford. The National Historic District preserves many fine buildings of the era, and the Whaling Museum gives accounts of the enterprise.

4 Plymouth
Massachusetts ■ **Routes 3 & 44**
■ **Visitor information:** 130 Water St; 1 508 747 7525 ■ www.seeplymouth.com

The first English settlement in New England, Plymouth is home to Plimoth Plantation, which recreates the lives of Massachusetts' and Wampanoag's earliest settlers. Explore *Mayflower II*, a replica of the 17th-century ship that brought the Pilgrims to the Americas. On Thanksgiving, the town celebrates with a parade in Pilgrim dress, while many Native American protesters observe a National Day of Mourning.

5 Salem
Massachusetts ■ **Route 1A**
■ **Visitor information:** 2 New Liberty St; 1 978 740 1650 ■ www.nps.gov/sama

Notorious for the trial and execution of "witches" in 1692, Salem is a vibrant city with a rich maritime history. Popular attractions include walking tours that recount the city's China Trade days (c. 1780–1880), and the Peabody Essex Museum – a leading interpreter of creative expressions from several cultures.

Facade of the Salem Witch Museum

Providence, Rhode Island

6 Providence
Rhode Island ■ Routes 1 or I-95 ■ Visitor information: 1 Sabin St; 1 401 751 1177 ■ www.goprovidence.com

Providence is a great walking city. Stroll Benefit Street's "mile of history" to see an impressive group of Colonial and Federal houses, or visit Waterplace Park with its pretty walkways along the Providence River. Atwells Avenue on Federal Hill is Providence's Little Italy, bustling with restaurants and cafés.

7 Lowell
Massachusetts ■ Routes I-93, I-95, & 3 ■ Visitor information: 246 Market St; 1 978 970 5000 ■ Boott Cotton Mills Museum: adm ■ www.nps.gov/lowe

Lowell was the cradle of the US's Industrial Revolution, where entrepreneurs dug power canals and built America's first textile mills on the Merrimack River. The sites within the National Historical Park tell parallel stories of a wrenching transformation from an agricultural to industrial lifestyle. A 1920s weave room still thunders away at Boott Cotton Mills Museum.

8 Old Sturbridge Village
Massachusetts
■ Routes I-90, 20, & 84 ■ Visitor Center: 1 Sturbridge Village Rd; 800 733 1830 ■ www.osv.org

Interpreters in period costumes go about their daily lives in a typical 1830s New England village. This large living history museum has more than 40 buildings on 0.3 sq miles (0.8 sq km). Visitors can get a sense of the era at the village common, mill district, and the farm.

9 Portsmouth
New Hampshire ■ Routes 1 or I-95 ■ Visitor information: 500 Market St; 1 603 610 5510 ■ www.goportsmouthnh.com

Founded in 1623 as Strawbery Banke, the historic houses on Marcy Street document three centuries of city life from earliest settlement through to 20th-century immigration. Picturesque shops, pubs, and restaurants surround Market Square and line the waterfront, and the surrounding streets house fine examples of Federal architecture.

10 Newport
Rhode Island ■ Routes I-93, 24, & 114 ■ Visitor information: 21 Long Wharf Mall; 1 401 845 9123 ■ www.discovernewport.org

Newport has been a playground for the rich since the late 1860s. Many of the elaborate "cottages" built by 19th-century industrialists are open for tours, including Breakers on Ochre Point Avenue. For natural beauty, hike the 3.6-mile (5.5-km) Cliff Walk overlooking Narragansett Bay and Easton's Beach.

TOP 10 Day Trips: The Beach

1 Cape Ann
Routes I-95 & 127 ▪ **Visitor information: 33 Commercial St, Gloucester; 1 978 283 1601**

Thirty miles (48 km) north of Boston, the granite jaw of Cape Ann juts defiantly into the Atlantic – a rugged landscape of precipitous cliffs and deeply cleft harbors. In Gloucester, a waterfront statue and plaque memorialize the 10,000 local fishermen who have perished at sea since 1623, and the Cape Ann Museum displays maritime paintings. The picturesque harborfront of Rockport is an artists' enclave and is lined with galleries.

Sunset at Gloucester, Cape Ann

2 Upper Cape Cod
Routes 3, 6, & 28

The Upper Cape is tranquil and low-key. Visitors can watch the boats glide through Cape Cod Canal or take the Shining Sea bikeway from Falmouth village to Woods Hole. If it's beaches you seek, Sandwich's Sandy Neck has dunes and excellent bird-watching, but Falmouth's Surf Drive is best for swimmers and Old Silver Beach is great for sunset views.

Boats at Nantucket Island's harbor

3 Mid Cape Cod
Routes 3, 6, & 28

The Mid Cape tends to be congested, especially in the town of Hyannis. But the north shore can be peaceful, with amazing wildlife and stunning views, especially from Gray's Beach in Yarmouth. Warmer water and sandy strands line the south side of Mid Cape, with especially good swimming in Harwich and Dennisport. There's also excellent canoeing and kayaking on the Bass River.

4 Outer Cape Cod
Routes 3 & 6 ▪ **www.nps.gov/caco**

Here you'll find some of the area's best beaches. The 40-mile (64-km) National Seashore offers great surfing at Coast Guard and Nauset Light, and the beaches of Marconi, Head of the Meadow, and Race Point all have dramatic dunes and great ocean swimming. The artist colonies of Wellfleet and Truro are worth a visit as is Provincetown, a fishing village turned LGBTQ+ resort.

5 Nantucket Island
Routes 3 & 6 to Hyannis ▪ **Ferry to Nantucket: 1 508 477 8600** ▪ **Visitor information: Zero Main St, Nantucket; 1 508 228 1700; www.nantucketchamber.org**

The Whaling Museum in Nantucket tells the tale of the Quaker whalers who made the island prosperous in the 19th century. It now houses trophy beach houses and million-dollar yachts. Visitors can enjoy activities such as kayaking, casting

for striped bass from Surfside Beach, or cycling to the village of Sconset with its rose-covered clifftop cottages.

Gay Head Cliffs, Martha's Vineyard

6 Martha's Vineyard

Routes 3 & 28 to Woods Hole ■ **Ferry to Vineyard Haven: 1 508 477 8600** ■ **Visitor information: 24 Beach St, Vineyard Haven; 1 508 693 0085; www.mvy.com**

From Vineyard Haven it's a short drive to Oak Bluffs, with its ginger-bread cottages and historic carousel. Venture south to Edgartown and the 19th-century homes of rich whaling captains. Nearby, the 3-mile (5-km) Katama Beach is a magnet for sun worshipers. Southwest of the island is Menemsha, a picturesque fishing village and Aquinnah's Gay Head Cliffs which offer dramatic hiking routes.

7 Ipswich

Routes 95, 128, & 133, or 1A ■ **Visitor information: 36 South Main St; 1 978 356 8540; www.historicipswich.org**

Crane Beach in Ipswich is one of New England's most scenic, with over 4 miles (6.5 km) of white sand, warm water, and outstanding bird-watching. Also on the Crane Estate, you can visit Castle Hill mansion and its lovely Italianate gardens.

8 Newburyport

Routes I-95 & 1 ■ **Visitor information: 38R Merrimac St; 1 978 462 6680**

In the 19th century, Newburyport was a prosperous seaport. The grand three-story mansions along High Street present a virtual case study in Federal architecture, while boutiques and antiques shops line downtown Merrimac, Water, and State streets. The Parker River National Wildlife Refuge on the adjacent Plum Island is one of the US's top bird-watching sanctuaries, with sandpipers, egrets, and piping plovers among its many residents and visitors.

9 Revere Beach

Routes 1 & 1A ■ **"T" station: Revere Beach/Wonderland**

Established in 1896, Revere Beach was the first public beach in the US. Thanks to a centennial restoration, it's also one of the best, with nearly 3 miles (4.5 km) of clean white sand and clear blue water.

10 Hampton & Rye Beaches

Routes I-95, NH 101, & 1A ■ **Visitor information: 160 Ocean Blvd, Hampton Beach; 1 603 926 8717; www.hamptonbeach.org**

The New Hampshire coast just south of Portsmouth has extensive sandy beaches. Wallis Sands State Park is ideal for swimming but the best of the rocky overlooks is Rye's Ragged Neck Point picnic area. The party scene is at Hampton Beach. Odiorne Point State Park in Rye has picnic areas and walking trails.

Boston
Area by Area

Brick-built row houses in
Boston's historic North End

📻 Beacon Hill

With its elegant, 19th-century row houses, friendly grocers, pricey antiques shops, and hidden gardens, Beacon Hill screams "old money" like no other area in Boston. The most exclusive block in the district is the genteel Louisburg Square, which was modeled after London's Georgian residential squares. Throughout the 19th century and well into the 20th, the charming

Nichols House Museum exhibit

Beacon Hill was a veritable checkerboard of communities – segregated though they were. Sadly, little of Beacon Hill's diversity has survived its inevitable gentrification, but visitors to the city can still experience the neighborhood's myriad pasts inside its opulent mansions and humble schoolhouses, and along its enchanting cobblestone streets.

Louisburg Square on Beacon Hill

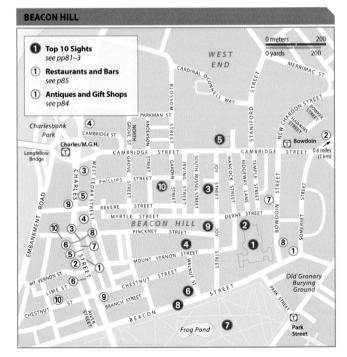

BEACON HILL

1 Top 10 Sights
see pp81–3

1 Restaurants and Bars
see p85

1 Antiques and Gift Shops
see p84

Gleaming dome and classical facade of the Massachusetts State House

1 Massachusetts State House

MAP P3 ■ 24 Beacon St ■ 617 727 3676 ■ Tours 10am–3:30pm Mon–Fri (reservations recommended) ■ www.sec.state.ma.us/trs

Curious eccentricities such as a colonial-era codfish, a stained-glass image of a Native American in a grass skirt, and a 23-carat gold dome crowned with a pine cone fill the interiors of Beacon Hill's most prestigious address (see p15).

2 Freedom Trail

MAP P4

The Freedom Trail (see pp12–13) was established in the 1950s to provide visitors with a connect-the-dots guide to Boston's colonial-era sites. It runs from Beacon Hill through Downtown, into the North End, and across the Charles River to Charlestown, which is the site of the famous warship USS *Constitution* and the Bunker Hill Monument.

3 Museum of African American History

MAP N2 ■ 46 Joy St ■ 617 725 0022 ■ Open 10am–4pm Mon–Sat ■ Adm ■ www.maah.org

Based in the African Meeting House (the oldest extant Black church in the US) and the adjoining Abiel Smith School (the first publicly funded grammar school for African American children in the country), the MAAH offers a look into the daily life of free, pre-Civil War African Americans. The meeting house was a political and religious center for Boston's African American community and it was here that abolitionists such as Frederick Douglass and William Lloyd Garrison delivered anti-slavery addresses in the mid-19th century. The museum has successfully preserved their legacy and that of countless others through its wide and fascinating range of workshops, exhibitions, and special events.

4 Nichols House Museum

MAP N3 ■ 55 Mount Vernon St ■ 617 227 6993 ■ Open Apr–Oct: Tue–Sat; Nov–Mar: Thu–Sat ■ Tours 11am–3pm ■ Adm ■ www.nichols housemuseum.org

An 1804 Charles Bulfinch design, this house is one of the earliest examples of residential architecture on Beacon Hill. Rose Nichols, the house's principal occupant for 75 years, bequeathed her home to the city as a museum, providing a glimpse of late 19th- and early 20th-century life on the Hill. A pioneering force for women in the arts and sciences, Nichols gained fame through her writings on landscape architecture and her philanthropic projects.

Skaters enjoying the Frog Pond on Boston Common

⑤ Harrison Gray Otis House

MAP N2 ▪ 141 Cambridge St
▪ 617 994 5920 ▪ Open Apr–Nov:
11am–4:30pm Wed–Sun ▪ Adm
▪ www.historicnewengland.org

One of the principal developers of Beacon Hill, Harrison Gray Otis (see p44), served in the Massachusetts legislature and gained a reputation for living the high life in this 1796 Bulfinch-designed mansion. Like a post-revolutionary Gatsby, Otis ensured his parties were the social events of the year. After falling into disrepair, the property was acquired in 1916 by the historical preservation society and has been restored to its original grandeur.

⑥ Parkman House

MAP N3 ▪ 33 Beacon St
▪ Closed to the public

George Parkman – once a prominent physician at Harvard Medical School – lived in this house during the mid-19th century. In 1849, in one of the most sensationalized murder cases in US history, Parkman was killed over a financial dispute. Both the crime and its aftermath were grisly – the ensuing trial saw the inclusion of dental records as evidence for the first time, as Parkman had been partially cremated. The house is now a city-owned meeting center.

⑦ Boston Common

The oldest city park (see pp18–19) in the country, the Common is a popular gathering place for outdoor concerts, public protests, picnics in summer and, in the winter, ice-skating on Frog Pond.

⑧ Beacon Street

MAP N3 ▪ Boston Athenaeum: 10½ Beacon St ▪ 617 227 0270 ▪ Open to the public noon–8pm Tue, 10am–4pm Wed–Sat ▪ Tours Tue, Thu & Sat by reservation ▪ Adm

Located in the blocks between Somerset and Brimmer streets, Beacon Street features the National

BLACK HERITAGE TRAIL

By and large, America's history books are dominated by white patriots such as Paul Revere and John Adams. As a refreshing counterpoint, the Black Heritage Trail posits that Black Bostonians, despite their marginalized histories, have played an indispensable role in the city's development. The trail illustrates this point at every turn, taking visitors past the homes and businesses of some of Boston's most influential Black Americans. Tours leave from the Shaw Memorial at 10am and 1pm from July to Labor Day and at 1pm from Labor Day to mid-October. Call a day ahead to book (617 742 5415; www.nps.gov/boaf).

Historic Landmark Boston Athenaeum, one of the oldest independent libraries in the country, housed in a sumptuous building containing a collection of over 600,000 titles. Also here are the Massachusetts State House (see p81), Parkman House, and the Third Harrison Gray Otis House, at 45 Beacon St, considered architect Charles Bulfinch's finest Federal-style house. The facade of the former Bull and Finch Pub is famed as the exterior of the bar in the TV show *Cheers*.

Boston Athenaeum library

(9) George Middleton House
MAP N3 ■ 5–7 Pinckney St
■ Closed to the public

The oldest remaining private residence on Beacon Hill built by African Americans is a highlight of the Black Heritage Trail. George Middleton, a Revolutionary War veteran, commissioned the house's construction soon after the war. Legend has it that he commanded an all-black company dubbed the "Bucks of America."

(10) Boston's Center for Jewish Culture
MAP N2 ■ 13–18 Phillips St ■ 617 523 2324 ■ Open 11am–5pm Wed–Fri ■ www.vilnashul.org

The Vilna Shul testifies to the area's former vibrancy as Boston's first predominantly Jewish quarter. The congregation was founded in 1903 by immigrants who came from Vilna, Lithuania. It is now a center of Jewish culture with programs and exhibits.

BEACON HILL BY DAY

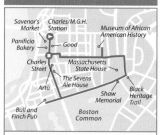

▶ MORNING

Take the "T" to the Charles Street/Massachusetts General Hospital stop and exit onto **Charles Street** (see p69). Enjoy a light breakfast at **Panificio Bakery** (144 Charles St) where the scones and muffins are out of this world. Then continue along Charles Street and turn right onto Beacon Street for a glimpse of the former **Bull and Finch Pub** (84 Beacon St), the bar that inspired the TV show *Cheers*. Continue up Beacon to the **Massachusetts State House** (see p81) for a free 45-minute weekday tour; hours vary. Afterward, cross the road to the **Shaw Memorial** (see p18), from where National Park ranger-led **Black Heritage Trail** tours depart. The trail provides an excellent survey of the area's architectural styles as well as its Black culture sites, and concludes at the **Museum of African American History** (see p81).

AFTERNOON

Walk back down the hill to Charles Street for a fortifying late lunch. Weather permitting, stock up on fresh fruit, a crusty baguette, and a sampling of imported cheeses at the charming **Savenor's Market** (160 Charles St) and have a picnic on **Boston Common**. Or, for diner-style fare, try sandwiches and bowls at the **Paramount** (see p85). After lunch, peruse the classy paper goods at **Rugg Road** (105 Charles St) and browse Charles Street's antique shops (see p84). Round the day off with a pint at **The Sevens Ale House** (see p85).

See map on p80 ←

Antiques and Gift Shops

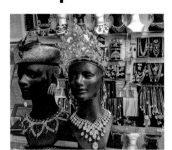

Jewelry at 20th Century Limited

1 20th Century Limited
MAP M3 ■ 73 Charles St

Specialists in vintage costume jewelry, 20th Century also offers handsome 1950s barware, classic accessories, and other collectibles.

2 Eugene Galleries
MAP M3 ■ 76 Charles St ■ Closed Sun & Mon

This shop has an excellent and fascinating selection of antique books, maps, and prints, many of which depict the development and history of Boston.

3 Beacon Hill Chocolates
MAP M3 ■ 91 Charles St

Handmade boxes of artisan chocolates, decorated with vintage Boston scenes, make ideal gifts. Don't miss the signature swirl of Caramel Sushi.

4 Rugg Road Paper Company
MAP M3 ■ 105 Charles St

Beacon Hill Chocolates

A treasure trove for all stationery lovers, the Rugg Road Paper Company is located in historic Beacon Hill. Reflecting elegant style and sophistication, this paper company offers novelty items such as handmade paper, cards, gift items, and personalized stationery.

5 Boston Art & Antiques Company
MAP M3 ■ 119 Charles St

Twelve dealers operate in this space filled with treasures including Asian antiques, sculptures, estate jewelry, tableware, paintings, and much more.

6 Blackstone's of Beacon Hill
MAP M3 ■ 46 Charles St ■ Closed Tue

This is the place to go for unique Boston-themed gifts such as *Make Way for Ducklings* pillows and ornaments, as well as high-quality Fenway Park mugs.

7 Elegant Findings
MAP M3 ■ 89 Charles St ■ Closed Tue, Wed & Sun

An intimate shop specializing in museum-quality, hand-painted 19th-century porcelain from all over Europe. You'll also find marble statuary, exquisite linens, and fine period furniture here.

8 Upstairs Downstairs
MAP M3 ■ 93 Charles St

A refreshing emphasis on affordability and function is placed at this cozy spot. Everything from mahogany four-poster beds to *belle époque* opera glasses is on display.

9 Marika's Antiques
MAP M3 ■ 130 Charles St ■ Closed Sun & Mon

Packed to its dusty rafters with oil paintings, tarnished silverware, and mismatched china – nothing quite beats that thrill of discovery you'll find here.

10 Helen's Leather
MAP M3 ■ 110 Charles St ■ Closed Tue

While many Beacon Hill shops evoke the city's elite past, Helen's flies the flag for casual western womenswear. The chic locals swear by it for smart and warm winter boots.

Restaurants and Bars

PRICE CATEGORIES

For a three course meal for one with half a bottle of wine (or equivalent meal), taxes, and extra charges.

$ under $40 $$ $40–$60 $$$ over $60

1 Mooo
MAP P3 ■ 15 Beacon St
■ 617 670 2515 ■ $$$

Mooo specializes in extraordinary beef and classic accompaniments at expense-account prices. The wine list includes many stellar names.

2 City Winery
MAP G3 ■ 80 Beverly St
■ 617 933 8047 ■ $$

This stylish wine bar (see p61) boasts an on-site winery, a shop, and a concert space which hosts live music performances every night.

3 Beacon Hill Pub
MAP M2 ■ 149 Charles St
■ 617 523 1895

A popular cash-only, no-frills bar that represents a holdout of pre-gentrification on Beacon Hill. Beer flows freely and patrons adore the foosball table and arcade games.

4 Alibi
MAP F3 ■ Liberty Hotel, 215 Charles St ■ 857 241 1144 ■ $$$

Located within the Liberty Hotel, the trendy Alibi (see p61) is a good spot for cocktails. The hotel also houses Scampo, a chic restaurant with a modern Italian-accented menu.

5 The Sevens Ale House
MAP M3 ■ 77 Charles St

The epitome of a local Boston bar, with dark wood, slightly surly staff, amiable patrons, a dartboard, and a rudimentary pub menu.

6 Paramount
MAP M3 ■ 44 Charles St
■ 617 720 1152 ■ Open daily ■ $

Paramount is reliably good at any time of day. Breakfast calls for diner-style egg classics, lunch focuses on burgers, and dinner is all about sizzling grill fare.

7 Grotto
MAP N3 ■ 37 Bowdoin St
■ 617 227 3434 ■ Closed L ■ $$

A cozy Beacon Hill fixture serving Italian-style fixed-price menus. Order a pasta dish – you won't regret it.

8 21st Amendment
MAP G3 ■ 150 Bowdoin St

This neighborhood pub near the State House is a classy spot for legislators to indulge in a tipple or two.

The 21st Amendment pub

9 Toscano
MAP M3 ■ 47 Charles St ■ 617 723 4090 ■ Closed L Mon–Fri ■ $$

Toscano pioneered Tuscan cooking in Beacon Hill. The restaurant's venerable kitchen works wonders with charcoal-grilled meats.

10 75 Chestnut
MAP M3 ■ 75 Chestnut St
■ 617 227 2175 ■ Closed L except Sat & Sun brunch ■ $$

Set in a converted townhouse, this restaurant serves as one of Beacon Hill's most popular hangouts for brunch and dinner. The menu offers affordable American bistro dishes.

See map on p80

 Back Bay

The easily navigated grid of streets in Back Bay bears little resemblance to the labyrinthine lanes around Downtown and the North End. In the mid-1800s, Back Bay was filled in to accommodate Boston's mushrooming population and, by the late 1800s, the area had become a vibrant, upscale neighborhood. Home to many of Boston's wealthiest families, the area was characterized by lavish houses, grand churches, and bustling commercial zones. Many of the original buildings stand intact, providing an exquisite 19th-century backdrop for today's pulsing nightlife, world-class shopping, and sumptuous dining.

Interior of Boston Public Library

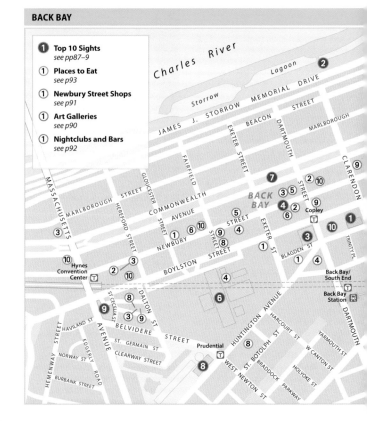

BACK BAY

1 **Top 10 Sights**
see pp87–9

1 **Places to Eat**
see p93

1 **Newbury Street Shops**
see p91

1 **Art Galleries**
see p90

1 **Nightclubs and Bars**
see p92

1 Trinity Church

When Henry Cobb's 60-story John Hancock Tower was completed in 1976, Bostonians feared that Trinity Church (see pp32–3) would be over-shadowed by its gleaming neighbor. Yet H. H. Richardson's masterpiece, dedicated in 1877, remains just as vital to Copley Square, and as beautiful, as it was on its opening day.

2 The Esplanade
MAP M3

The perfect setting for a leisurely bike ride, invigorating jog, or a lazy afternoon of soaking up the sun, the Esplanade is one of the city's most popular green spaces. This ribbon of green hugging the Charles' river-banks was inspired by Venetian

Charles' bank along the Esplanade

canals. The Esplanade is at its busiest on the Fourth of July (see p73), when the world-famous Boston Pops Orchestra plays at the Hatch Shell and thousands of revelers flock here to enjoy the incomparable mix of music, good cheer, and awe-inspiring fireworks.

3 Boston Public Library
MAP L5 ■ 700 Boylston St ■ 617 536 5400 ■ Open 9am–9pm Mon–Thu, 9am–5pm Fri & Sat, 1–5pm Sun ■ Tours 2:30pm Mon, 6pm Tue & Thu, 11am Wed, Fri & Sat, 2pm Sun ■ www.bpl.org

Founded in 1848 as America's first fully public library, the Boston Public Library moved into its current location in 1895. The building, designed by McKim, Mead, & White, has lavish stone and marble interiors, gleaming oak woodwork, and murals by leading artists of the era on its walls. No wonder it's been called a "palace of the people." Take a guided tour to learn more about the building's architecture and history. Note that the courtyard restaurant serves afternoon tea.

4 Newbury Street

Over the years, Back Bay's most famous street (see pp24–5) has proven to be amazingly adaptable, with fashion boutiques blending seam-lessly into their mid-19th-century brownstone environs. This is the liveliest, most eclectic street in Boston: skateboarders glide along-side catwalk models, and delivery trucks and Ferraris jockey for the same parking space. Expect to hear a dozen languages on the sidewalks.

5 Gibson House Museum

MAP M4 ▪ 137 Beacon St ▪ 617 267 6338 ▪ Tours 1pm, 2pm & 3pm Wed–Sun ▪ Adm ▪ www.the gibsonhouse.org

One of the first private residences to be built in Back Bay (c. 1859), Gibson House remains beautifully intact. It has been preserved as a monument to the era, thanks largely to the efforts of its final resident (the grandson of the woman who built the house). So frozen in time does this house appear that you might feel like you're intruding on someone's inner sanctum, and an earlier age. Highlights of the tour include elegant porcelain dinnerware, 18th-century heirloom jewelry, and exquisite black walnut woodwork throughout the house. During Pride month (June), the museum often runs tours dedicated to the life of the house's last owner – writer Charles Gibson.

6 Prudential Center

MAP K6 ▪ 800 Boylston St ▪ 617 236 3100 ▪ Stores open 10am–9pm Mon–Sat, 11am–7pm Sun

The Prudential Tower's 52 stories seem dwarfed by the huge swath of street-level shops and restaurants that constitute the Prudential Center. With its indoor shopping mall, restaurants, supermarket, cluster of residential towers, and massive convention center, the Prudential Center is like a self-contained city within a city. It is linked via a skywalk over Huntington Avenue to the Copley Place shopping and hotel complex.

Statues on Commonwealth Avenue

7 Commonwealth Avenue

MAP J5–L4

With its leafy pedestrian mall and *belle époque*-inspired architecture, Commonwealth Avenue aptly deserves its comparison to *les rues parisiennes*. A morning jog on the mall is a popular pastime, as is the occasional picnic or afternoon snooze on a bench. Highlights include Boston's First Baptist Church *(110 Commonwealth; open for worship)* and the pedestrian mall's stately statues, including the William Lloyd Garrison bronze, sculpted by Olin Levi Warner.

8 Christian Science Center

MAP K6 ▪ 175 Huntington Ave ▪ 617 450 7000 ▪ Exhibits open 10am–5pm daily ▪ Adm for Mapparium ▪ www.marybakereddylibrary.org

While believers head for the Romanesque-Byzantine basilica, the library (entered from Massachusetts Avenue) emphasizes inspirational facets of the life of the founder *(see pp44–5)* rather than church doctrine.

Christian Science Center and the Prudential Center

The Mapparium, a walk-through stained-glass globe with 1935 political boundaries, remains the most popular exhibit (see p50), but don't miss the Neo-Classical lobby of the *Christian Science Monitor*. Outside, a 670-ft (204-m) reflecting pool, designed by I. M. Pei, is lined with begonias, marigolds, and columbines.

⑨ Berklee Performance Center

MAP J6 ▪ 136 Massachusetts Ave ▪ 617 747 2261 ▪ Check website for details of concerts and performances ▪ www.berklee.edu/BPC

The largest independent music school in the world, Berklee was founded in 1945. The college has produced a number of world-renowned jazz, rock, and pop stars, including Quincy Jones, Melissa Etheridge, Kevin Eubanks, Jan Hammer, and Branford Marsalis. The state-of-the-art performance center hosts concerts by students, faculty, and visiting artists.

⑩ Copley Square

MAP L5

Named after John Singleton Copley, the renowned 18th-century Boston painter, Copley Square is surrounded by some of the city's most striking architectural gems, notably Trinity Church and the Boston Public Library. A hub of activities, the bustling square hosts weekly farmers' markets, concerts, and folk dance shows in summer. The BosTix booth sells discounted tickets for theater, music, and dance performances.

▶ AFTERNOON

Enjoy a *croque monsieur* or *moules frites* at the **Bistro du Midi** (272 Boylston St) while gazing out onto the **Public Garden** (see pp18–19). Stroll one block over to **Newbury Street** (see p87) and take in the impressive contemporary art galleries concentrated between Arlington and Dartmouth streets. Then cross back over to Boylston at Dartmouth and sit for a while inside **Trinity Church** (see p87) where La Farge's stained-glass windows top an inexhaustible list of highlights. And while you're in an aesthetics-appreciating mood, traverse St. James Place to the **Fairmont Copley Plaza** hotel (see p148) and lounge for a few moments in the ornate, Versailles-esque lobby. Next, cross Dartmouth to the **Boston Public Library** (see p87) and admire John Singer Sargent's gorgeous murals.

Now it's time to warm up your credit card, so head back to Newbury Street for a dizzying shopping spree. Turn left onto Newbury for Boston-only boutiques such as **Newbury Comics** (see p91) and **Trident Booksellers & Café** (see p91). Pause for a reinvigorating fruit smoothie or towering sundae at **Ben & Jerry's** (174 Newbury St). At Massachusetts Avenue, turn left, then left again onto Boylston and continue to the **Prudential Center** for name-brand shopping – you'll find Saks Fifth Avenue, Lord & Taylor, and the like. Cap it all off with a bracing-cold cocktail in the elegant surroundings of the City Bar (see p92) in the Lenox Hotel, an Edwardian-era survivor just a block away on Exeter Street.

See map on pp86–7

Art Galleries

1 Robert Klein
MAP M5 ■ 38 Newbury St
■ 617 267 7997 ■ Closed Sun & Mon

Everybody who's anybody in photography vies for space at Robert Klein. Past coups include shows by Annie Leibovitz and Herb Ritts.

2 Copley Society of Art
MAP L5 ■ 158 Newbury St
■ 617 536 5049 ■ Closed Mon

With a commitment to exhibiting works by promising New England artists, this non-profit organization has been providing young artists with that crucial first break since 1879.

3 Childs Gallery
MAP TK ■ 169 Newbury St ■ 617 266 1108 ■ Closed Mon

The Childs Gallery was founded in 1937 and displays an eclectic range of paintings, drawings and sculpture. Don't miss the print department in the basement.

4 Krakow Witkin Gallery
MAP M5 ■ 10 Newbury St
■ 617 262 4490 ■ Closed Sun
& Mon; Aug

Since its opening in 1964, this gallery has championed contemporary artists who create conceptually driven and minimalist work.

Work by Jackie Ferrara, Krakow Witkin Gallery

5 DTR Modern Galleries
MAP L5 ■ 167 Newbury St
■ 617 424 9700

DTR champions modern and contemporary art with an inventory that ranges from Salvador Dalí to Andy Warhol.

6 Guild of Boston Artists
MAP L5 ■ 162 Newbury St
■ 617 536 7660 ■ Closed Sun & Mon

The skylit gallery space houses representational paintings and sculptures by New England artists. More than 40 artists founded the guild in 1914.

7 Vose Galleries
MAP K5 ■ 238 Newbury St ■ 617 536 6176 ■ Closed Sun & Mon

The oldest art gallery in the US, Vose specializes in American realist paintings and works on paper from the 18th–20th centuries.

Sculpture outside Vose Galleries

8 Pucker Gallery
MAP K5 ■ 240 Newbury St, 3rd floor ■ 617 267 9473

You never know what you might discover in this gallery that embraces work in a variety of media created by US and international artists.

9 Gallery NAGA
MAP M5 ■ 67 Newbury St
■ 617 267 9060 ■ Closed Sun & Mon; Jul & Aug

Representing some of New England's best regarded artists, NAGA is possibly Newbury's top contemporary art gallery.

10 Arden Gallery
MAP L5 ■ 129 Newbury St
■ 617 247 0610 ■ Closed Sun

This gallery focuses on original paintings and sculpture, including those cast in bronze and other metals. It also showcases up-and-coming abstract and realist artists.

Newbury Street Shops

① Johnny Cupcakes
MAP K6 ■ 279 Newbury St

This boutique specializes in limited-edition crossbones-and-cupcake T-shirts. The joke continues with bakery case displays, aprons on the staff, and the smell of cake batter in the air.

② Trident Booksellers & Café
MAP K6 ■ 338 Newbury St

Trident is popular for its delicious, healthy sandwiches, strong coffee concoctions, and what is arguably the best book and magazine selection in the city.

Display at Newbury Comics

③ Newbury Comics
MAP J6 ■ 348 Newbury St

Generally undercutting the chain stores on CDs, Newbury Comics delivers value along with a stellar selection of rare import CDs and a growing range of exclusive, rare and vintage vinyl, as well as concert videos, and the latest comics.

④ No Rest for Bridget
MAP K5 ■ 220 Newbury St

Youngsters flock to the Boston outpost of this Los Angeles womenswear label to pick up soft, effortless, and comfortable threads. It's a popular choice come spring break and summer vacation.

⑤ Hempest
MAP K5 ■ 301 Newbury St

A true believer in the superiority of hemp as something to wear rather than inhale, Hempest showcases chic and casual styles fashioned from this environmentally friendly fiber.

⑥ Boston Olive Oil Company
MAP K5 ■ 253 Newbury St

A family-owned shop, Boston Olive Oil Company offers more than 60 premium varieties of extra virgin olive oil and balsamic vinegars.

⑦ Shreve, Crump & Low
MAP M5 ■ 39 Newbury St ■ Closed Sun

First opened in 1796 near Paul Revere's silversmith shop, this fine jeweler is a Boston institution, renowned for its engagement rings. But the "gurgling cod" jugs make a whimsical and less pricey gift.

⑧ Concepts
MAP J6 ■ 73 Newbury St

An impressive collection of sneakers, street wear, and designer clothing, ranging from Adidas to Jimmy Choo is stocked here.

⑨ Simon Pearce
MAP F4 ■ 103 Newbury St

Fine blown glass and handmade pottery from this eponymous Irish designer and artist creates tableware with an upscale touch. Pearce signatures include classic goblets and other stemware.

⑩ Deluca's Back Bay Market
MAP K5 ■ 239 Newbury St

This grocer-meets-corner market stocks fabulous produce, chilled beer, ready-made sandwiches, and imported delights of all kinds.

See map on pp86–7

Nightclubs and Bars

1 City Bar
MAP F5 ▪ 65 Exeter St
▪ Open till 2am daily

The dark wood interior and leather seating make this glamorous room in the Lenox Hotel a sophisticated choice. City Bar also seems worlds away from the hubbub of Back Bay.

2 Oak Long Bar & Kitchen
MAP L6 ▪ 138 St James Ave

This award-winning bar (see p60) in the historic Copley Plaza (see p148) exudes old-school class and charm.

3 Kings
MAP J6 ▪ 50 Dalton St

The 1950s were never as cool as they seem at this retro-style lounge, pool hall, and bowling alley buried downstairs next to the Hynes Convention Center.

4 Bar 10
MAP F5 ▪ 10 Huntington Ave

The Westin Copley Place's lobby bar has cozy booths, perfect for a leisurely drink, while the high top tables are a great choice for quick sips and rendezvous.

5 M.J. O'Connor's
MAP F4 ▪ 27 Columbus Ave

Located in the Park Plaza Hotel, this expansive Irish-style pub features a full bar, complete with taps dripping with Guinness and several local brews. It serves comfort food, too.

6 The Street Bar
MAP F4 ▪ The Newbury, 1 Newbury St ▪ Closed 11:30pm or 12:30am Fri & Sat

Boston's elite have been socializing at this hideaway facing the Public Garden since the Prohibition ended.

7 Bijou Nightclub
MAP G5 ▪ 51 Stuart St

High rollers reserve a table at Bijou to enjoy a glass of champagne, but most of the crowd come to dance to the Latin and House beats.

8 Bukowski Tavern
MAP K6 ▪ 50 Dalton St

A beer drinker's paradise, Bukowski counts 100 varieties of the beverage. Its primary patrons are a professional crowd during the day and young hipsters at night.

9 Lolita Cocina & Tequila Bar
MAP L5 ▪ 271 Dartmouth St

There's always a festive mood at this trendy, Gothic-style bar. Choose from the long list of specialty tequilas, accompanied by Mexican food.

10 Dillon's
MAP K5 ▪ 955 Boylston St

Set in a former police station, Dillon's serves an all-American menu and drinks. The interior of this bi-level bar is impressive, but the outdoor patio is hard to beat in good weather.

Exterior of Dillon's bi-level bar

Places to Eat

PRICE CATEGORIES
For a three-course meal for one with half a bottle of wine (or equivalent meal), taxes, and extra charges.

$ under $40 **$$** $40–$60 **$$$** over $60

1 Sorellina
MAP F5 ▪ 1 Huntington Ave ▪ 617 412 4600 ▪ $$$
Regional Italian food with a contemporary spin is accompanied by a range of great wines in this sophisticated dining room.

2 Saltie Girl
MAP F4 ▪ 281 Dartmouth St ▪ 617 267 0691 ▪ $$$
Inspired by Barcelona's seafood bars, Saltie Girl offers delicious dishes made with local fish. The restaurant serves a variety of excellent cocktails.

3 Deuxave
MAP E5 ▪ 371 Commonwealth Ave ▪ 617 517 5915 ▪ Closed L ▪ $$$
Elegant contemporary dining ranges from local lobster and scallops to caramelized onion ravioli.

4 Eataly
MAP K6 ▪ 800 Boylston St ▪ 617 807 7300 ▪ $–$$$
This vast emporium of all things Italian includes more than a dozen different dining venues amid the groceries and kitchen gadgets.

5 Banks Fish House
MAP M5 ▪ 406 Stuart St ▪ 617 399 0015 ▪ Closed L Sat & Sun ▪ $$$
Order a cup of chowder or a glass of Chablis at the bar or opt for a seafood feast with dishes such as broiled lobster or herb-crusted halibut at this restaurant (see p65).

6 Mistral
MAP M6 ▪ 223 Columbus Ave ▪ 617 867 9300 ▪ $$$
Delectable French-Mediterranean dishes and an excellent wine list make Mistral an ideal dining venue.

Entrance to Grill 23 & Bar

7 Grill 23 & Bar
MAP M5 ▪ 161 Berkeley St ▪ 617 542 2255 ▪ Closed L ▪ $$$
Grill 23 harkens back to the days of exclusive, Prohibition-era supper clubs. Prime aged beef with an inventive spin is served in a sumptuously classic interior.

8 Lucie Drink + Dine
MAP K6 ▪ 120 Huntington Ave ▪ 617 425 3400 ▪ $$$
Serving everything from steak and fries to rice bowls, the Colonnade Hotel's stylish restaurant specializes in comfort food from around the globe.

9 Summer Shack
MAP K6 ▪ 50 Dalton St ▪ 617 867 9955 ▪ Closed Nov–Mar: L Mon–Fri ▪ $$
Chef Jasper White serves excellent dishes at the Summer Shack (see p65). Try the buttered lobster and corn.

10 Uni
MAP J5 ▪ 370A Commonwealth Ave ▪ 617 536 7200 ▪ Closed L & Mon ▪ $$$
Contemporary Japanese cuisine rules at this fine-dining *izakaya* restaurant. Late night weekend ramen draws a crowd.

See map on pp86–7

🔟 North End and the Waterfront

The North End is Boston's Italian village, where one feast day blends into the next all summer as the great-grandchildren of the original immigrants celebrate the music, food, and dolce vita of the old country. Yet the North End predates its Italian inhabitants and the neighborhood is in fact the oldest in Boston. The area along the waterfront bristles with condo developments on former shipping piers, which lead south to the bustle of Long, Central, and Rowes wharves. Boston was born by the sea and it is now reclaiming its waterfront as a vital center for business and pleasure.

Old North Church road marker

NORTH END AND THE WATERFRONT

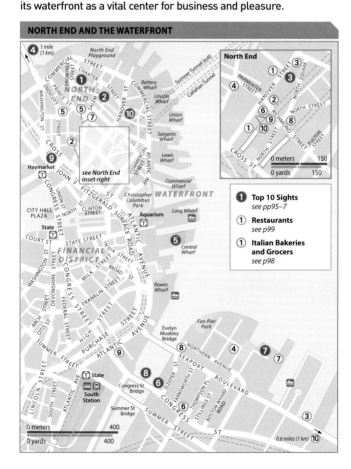

North End

0 meters 150
0 yards 150

1 mile (1 km)

0 meters 400
0 yards 400

0.6 miles (1 km)

1 **Top 10 Sights**
see pp95–7

1 **Restaurants**
see p99

1 **Italian Bakeries and Grocers**
see p98

1 Copp's Hill Burying Ground

MAP Q1 ■ Hull St ■ 617 635 4505
■ Open 9am–5pm daily

Trace the history of Boston on the thousands of tombstones found here (see p13), from the mean-spirited Mather family, who were theocrats who ruled the early city of the late 17th and 18th century, to the valiant patriots slain in the fight for freedom during the American Revolution. In the Battle of Bunker Hill (see p14), the British, who occupied the city in 1775, manned a battery from this site and fired on neighboring Charlestown. There are sweeping views of the harbor.

2 Old North Church

MAP Q1 ■ 193 Salem St ■ 617 858 8231 ■ Open Apr–Nov: 9am–6pm daily (shorter hours off-season) ■ Adm ■ www.oldnorth.com

An active Episcopal congregation still worships at Boston's oldest church (see p13), officially known as Christ Church (1723). It was here, in 1775, that sexton Robert Newman hung two lanterns in the belfry to warn horseback messenger Paul Revere of British troop movements, an event commemorated by a bronze plaque in the street outside.

Exterior of Paul Revere House

3 Paul Revere House

MAP Q1 ■ 19 North Sq
■ 617 523 2338 ■ Open mid-Apr–Oct: 9:30am–5:15pm daily; Nov–mid-Apr: 9:30am–4:15pm daily (closed Mon Jan–Mar) ■ Adm
■ www.paulreverehouse.org

Home to Paul Revere for 30 years, this 17th-century clapboard house (see p13) is the only surviving home of any of Boston's revolutionary heroes. It provides an intriguing glimpse into the domestic life of Revere's family with displays of their furniture and possessions, including silverwork made by Revere, who was highly regarded as a metalsmith. Well-trained staff tell the tale of Revere's legendary midnight ride (see p14).

4 Charlestown Navy Yard

MAP H2

One of the original six naval yards created to support the fledgling US Navy, the Charlestown Navy Yard (see pp36–7) was a center of technical innovation. The heart of the yard opened as a historic site in 1974. Its two most popular exhibits include the famous USS *Constitution* frigate, and the World War II-era destroyer USS *Cassin Young*.

5 New England Aquarium

Now the centerpiece of the downtown waterfront development, the aquarium (see pp38–9) was constructed in the 1960s and paved the way for the revitalization of Boston Harbor. Harbor seals cavort in a tank in front of the sleek structure.

Interior of Old North Church

Exterior of the Children's Museum

6 Children's Museum

MAP R5 ■ 308 Congress St ■ 617 426 6500 ■ Open 10am–5pm daily (to 9pm Fri) ■ Adm ■ www. bostonchildrensmuseum.org

This interactive museum *(see p52)* is the perfect place to take the family for hands-on fun.

7 Institute of Contemporary Art

25 Harbor Shore Dr ■ 617 478 3100 ■ Open 10am–5pm Tue, Wed, Sat & Sun, 10am–9pm Thu & Fri ■ Adm ■ www.icaboston.org

The ICA was founded in 1936 and reopened in its modern landmark structure on Fan Pier in 2006. The striking glass, wood, and steel building, designed by Diller Scofidio + Renfro, is cantilevered over the HarborWalk and provides dramatic views. The ICA promotes cutting-edge art and focuses on 21st-century work. There is also a program of performing arts and other events, with waterfront concerts in summer.

8 Boston Tea Party Ships and Museum

MAP R5 ■ Congress St Bridge ■ 617 338 1773 ■ Open Apr–Oct: 10am–5pm daily (to 4pm in winter) ■ Adm ■ www.bostonteapartyship.com

The historic occasion known as the Boston Tea Party, when patriots dressed as Native Americans and threw a consignment of English tea overboard to protest against the Stamp Tax of 1773, proved to be a catalyst of the American Revolution *(see p14)*. The Boston Tea Party ships are replicas of the vessels that were relieved of their cargo that fateful December night. Costumed story-tellers recount events in rousing detail, and visitors can board one of the vessels and even participate in a re-enactment of the destruction. In the museum is one of two tea crates known to have survived from the incident, while Abigail's Tea Room serves up a nice "cuppa."

Harborside setting of the Boston Tea Party Ships and Museum

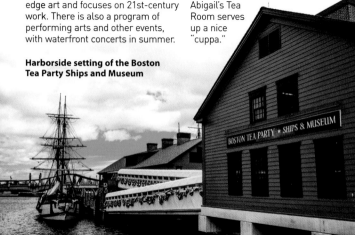

9 Rose Kennedy Greenway

MAP P1 ■ www.rosekennedy
greenway.org

The Greenway is a ribbon of organic, contemporary parkland through the heart of Boston, where visitors and locals laze on the lawns, cool off in the fountains, buy lunch at one of the affordable food trucks, and enjoy seasonal beer and wine gardens. There's a charming carousel featuring local hand-carved wildlife. Artworks include the Harbor Fog water sculpture, near Rowes Wharf, which evokes the sea with fog, light, and sound, as well as installations that change every year. Colorful garden plants punctuate the park's walkways.

Rose Kennedy Greenway

10 St. Stephen's Church

MAP R1 ■ 401 Hanover St ■ 617 523 1230 ■ Open 8:30am–4:30pm Mon–Sat, 11am Sun for worship

Renowned architect Charles Bulfinch completely redesigned St. Stephen's original 1714 structure in 1802–4, and the church is the only surviving example of his religious architecture. Its bell was cast by Paul Revere. The busy Neo-Classical exterior contrasts with the open, airy, and relatively unadorned interior. In 1862, the Roman Catholic archdiocese took over the church to accommodate the area's growing number of Irish immigrants. Rose Fitzgerald, daughter of Boston mayor and St. Stephen's parishioner John "Honey Fitz" Fitzgerald, and mother of President John F. Kennedy (see p45), is linked to the church. She was baptized here in 1890, and her funeral took place here in 1995.

FROM NARROW BYWAYS TO THE SEA

- Copp's Hill Burying Ground
- Langone Park
- Old North Church
- Caffè Vittoria
- Paul Revere House
- Joe's American Bar & Grill
- Haymarket Station
- New England Aquarium
- Rose Kennedy Greenway
- Boston Harbor Hotel
- Trade

525 yards (480 meters)

▶ MORNING

From the Haymarket "T", follow Hanover Street – the North End's principal artery – to Richmond Street and continue to North Square. Stop at **Paul Revere House** (see p95) for a glimpse into the domestic life of the revolutionary hero. Return to Hanover for an espresso at lively **Caffè Vittoria** (see p66). Continue up Hanover and turn left through Paul Revere Mall to **Old North Church** (see p95). Inside, the bust of George Washington is reputedly the world's most accurate rendering of his face – compare the resemblance to a dollar bill. Then stroll up Hull Street past **Copp's Hill Burying Ground** (see p95) for a great view of **USS Constitution** (see p36) and continue to the waterfront. Grab a bench in **Langone Park** (see p47) to watch a match of bocce. Walk south along Commercial Street and stop for an alfresco waterside lunch at **Joe's American Bar & Grill** (100 Atlantic Ave).

AFTERNOON

Resume your waterfront stroll, admiring the views of the harbor as you walk. Then stop off to enjoy the roses in the **Rose Kennedy Greenway**, before whiling away an hour or so in the **New England Aquarium** (see pp38–9) where highlights include the swirling Giant Ocean Tank. Relax with a sundowner on the patio of the **Boston Harbor Hotel** (see p146) before you head to **Trade** (see p99) for dinner and cocktails.

See map on p94

Italian Bakeries and Grocers

1 Mike's Pastry
MAP Q1 ▪ 300 Hanover St

Large glass cases display a huge selection of cookies and *cannoli* (crunchy pastry filled with a sweet ricotta cream). Purchase a box to go, or grab a table and order a drink and a delectable pastry.

2 Salumeria Italiana
MAP Q2 ▪ 151 Richmond St

This neighborhood fixture is a great source of esoteric Italian canned goods and rich olive oils, as well as spicy sausages and cheeses from many Italian regions.

3 The Wine Bottega
MAP Q2 ▪ 341 Hanover St

Run by wine connoisseurs, The Wine Bottega only stocks natural wines, which are made with no chemical input in the vineyard or the winery. The selection ranges from bargain-priced to ones that serve as an investment as well as some rare and delightful wines.

4 Polcari's Coffee Co.
MAP Q1 ▪ 105 Salem St
▪ Closed Sun

The premier bulk grocer in the North End, this charming store has sold fine Italian roasted coffee since 1932. It's still the best place to find spices, flours, grains, and legumes.

Coffee beans at Polcari's Coffee Co.

5 Bova's Bakery
MAP Q1 ▪ 134 Salem St

Head to Bova's Bakery for hot sandwiches, cookies, and bread, which is fresh and baked at all hours through the day.

6 Modern Pastry
MAP Q2 ▪ 257 Hanover St

Modern Pastry shop sign

The house specialties here include a rich ricotta pie, delicious florentines, and nougat, which are all made on the premises, as well as chocolate truffles from Italy. Some *cannoli* fans swear by Modern's delicate shells.

7 Monica's Mercato
MAP Q1 ▪ 130 Salem St

Linked to a nearby restaurant, this *salumeria* has all the usual cheeses and sausages, but its specialties are prepared foods such as cold salads for picnics and pasta dishes for reheating.

8 V. Cirace Wine & Spirits
MAP Q2 ▪ 173 North St
▪ Closed Sun

The North End's most upscale seller of Italian wines and liqueurs stocks both fine wines to lay down and cheerfully youthful ones to enjoy right away.

9 Bricco Panetteria
MAP Q2 ▪ 241 Hanover St

This subterranean bakery turns out amazing Italian and French breads day and night. Follow the delicious smells to find it tucked down an alley.

10 Bricco Salumeria & Pasta Shop
MAP Q2 ▪ 11 Board Alley

With many varieties of fresh pasta made daily, plus sauces, pesto, grating cheeses, and a handful of hard-to-find Italian groceries, this North End takeout is ideal for stocking up a picnic basket.

Restaurants

PRICE CATEGORIES
For a three-course meal for one with half a bottle of wine (or equivalent meal), taxes, and extra charges.

$ under $40 $$ $40–$60 $$$ over $60

1 Mare Oyster Bar
MAP H3 ■ 3 Mechanic St
■ 617 723 6273 ■ $$$

Savor Italian coastal cuisine at this sleek contemporary spot *(see p64)*, which offers a variety of crudos, a never-ending supply of oysters, and shellfish as well as some of the best organic white wines.

Seafood at Neptune Oyster

2 Neptune Oyster
MAP Q1 ■ 63 Salem St
■ 617 742 3474 ■ $$

The delicate raw bar oysters are almost upstaged by large and bold roasted fish and pasta dishes in this tiny, stylish spot. Tables turn quickly.

3 Legal Harborside
MAP H3 ■ Liberty Wharf and other locations ■ 617477 2900 ■ $$$

The flagship of the Legal Sea Foods chain, Legal Harborside offers three floors of seafood heaven. It's popular, so booking ahead is essential.

4 Strega Italiano Seaport
MAP H4 ■ 1 Marina Park Dr
■ 617 345 3992 ■ $$$

Italian by way of the Jersey Shore, this Tuscan steakhouse celebrates bold flavors and tannic red wines.

5 Pizzeria Regina
MAP Q1 ■ 11½ Thatcher St ■ $

Pizzeria Regina is a stalwart on Boston's pizzeria scene. This original, family-run branch bakes thin-crust, old-fashioned, Neapolitan-style pizzas in its brick oven.

6 Menton
MAP H5 ■ 354 Congress St
■ 617 737 0099 ■ Closed L ■ $$$

Barbara Lynch's luxurious restaurant *(see p63)* serves seasonally inspired dishes such as East Coast halibut, dry-aged ribeye, and crab bisque. Try the excellent four-course prix fixe menu or the chef's tasting menu.

7 Woods Hill Pier 4
MAP H4 ■ 300 Pier 4 Blvd
■ 617 981 4577 ■ Closed Mon, L Tue–Fri ■ $$$

Lending a creative twist to classic New England cuisine, this American chophouse uses ingredients fresh from its organic farm. It also offers unparalleled waterfront views.

8 Barking Crab
MAP H4 ■ 88 Sleeper St
■ 617 426 2722 ■ $$$

Located next to the Children's Museum, this casual waterfront restaurant *(see p64)* is one of the city's favourite spots for seafood and drinks.

9 Trade
MAP H4 ■ 540 Atlantic Ave
■ 617 451 1234 ■ $$$

This airy upscale restaurant *(see p62)* evokes Boston's global shipping days with its superb, eclectic world cuisine and creative cocktails.

10 Chickadee
21 Dry Dock Ave ■ 617 531 5591 ■ Closed Mon & Sun ■ $

A cheerful restaurant sporting a sleek and modern vibe. The menu abounds with light Mediterranean fare, such as octopus escabeche and slow-roasted *porchetta*.

See map on p94 ←

🔟 Downtown and the Financial District

The heart of Boston lies between Boston Common and the harbor. There are reminders of history embedded in the center of this metropolis. The 18th-century Old State House still shines within a canyon of skyscrapers. The heroes of Boston's early years – city founder John Winthrop, patriot Paul Revere, and revolutionary Samuel Adams – are buried just steps from sidewalks abuzz with shoppers. Rolled in to this area is the Financial District and Boston's oldest commercial district, Faneuil Hall Marketplace.

John Hancock's Grave, Old Granary Burying Ground

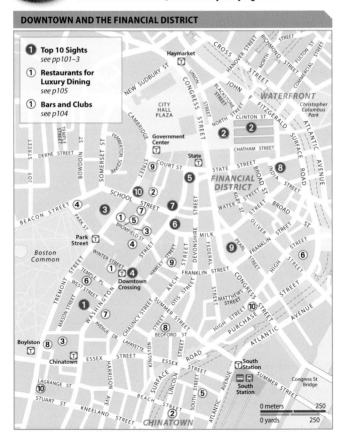

DOWNTOWN AND THE FINANCIAL DISTRICT

1 Top 10 Sights
see pp101–3

1 Restaurants for
Luxury Dining
see p105

1 Bars and Clubs
see p104

Brattle Book Shop, Ladder District

1 Ladder District
MAP P4

The network of short streets linking Washington and Tremont streets is today known as the Ladder District. Once derelict, the area is now filled with bars and restaurants. Anchoring the district are the Millennium Tower that overlooks Boston Common *(see pp18–19)*, the Ritz-Carlton, and the top-of-the-line AMC Boston Common cineplex *(175 Tremont St)*. A few stalwarts, such as landmark bookseller Brattle Book Shop, are holding out against the big guns.

2 Faneuil Hall Marketplace
MAP Q2 ■ 1 Faneuil Hall Sq ■ Open Faneuil Hall: 9am–5pm daily; Quincy Market: 10am–9pm Mon–Sat, 11am–7pm Sun (winter hours vary, check website) ■ www.faneuilhallmarket place.com

Faneuil Hall is a historic Boston landmark where, in the early to mid-18th century, enslaved people were auctioned. During the second half of the 18th century, this hall echoed with cries of revolution. The adjacent Quincy Market revolutionized Boston's food distribution in the 1820s. Today, the buildings and surrounding plazas form a shopping and dining hub called the Faneuil Hall Marketplace.

3 Old Granary Burying Ground
MAP P3 ■ Tremont St at Park St ■ 617 635 4505 ■ Open 9am–5pm daily

Dating from 1660, the Granary has the graves of many illustrious figures, including John Hancock, Samuel Adams, and Paul Revere *(see p44)*, who joined his revolutionary comrades here in 1818. There are other notables such as Declaration of Independence signatory Robert Treat Paine, parents of Benjamin Franklin, and Crispus Attucks – a freedom seeker who was the first casualty of the Boston Massacre *(see p14)*.

4 Downtown Crossing
MAP P4 ■ Junction of Summer, Winter & Washington Sts

This pedestrian-friendly shopping area is dominated by Macy's department store. Pushcart vendors offer more quirky goods, and food carts provide quick lunches for Downtown office workers.

5 Old State House
MAP Q3 ■ Washington & State Sts ■ 617 720 1713 ■ Open 9am–5pm daily (late May–early Sep: to 6pm) ■ Adm ■ www.bostonhistory.org

Built in 1713 as the seat of colonial government, the Old State House was sited to look down State Street. In 1770, the Boston Massacre *(see p14)* occurred outside its doors, and on July 18, 1776, the Declaration of Independence was first read from its balcony. Today, it's home to the Bostonian Society and Old State House Museum.

The colonial-era Old State House

Historic facade of Old South Meeting House

6 Old South Meeting House

MAP Q3 ▪ 310 Washington St
▪ 617 482 6439 ▪ Open Apr–Oct:
9:30am–5pm daily; Nov–Mar:
10am–4pm daily ▪ Adm ▪ www.
oldsouthmeetinghouse.org

Old South's rafters have rung with many impassioned speeches exhorting the overthrow of the king, the abolition of slavery, women's right to vote, an end to apartheid, and many other causes. Nearly abandoned when its congregation moved to Back Bay in 1876, it was saved in one of Boston's first acts of preservation.

7 Old Corner Bookstore

MAP P3 ▪ 1 School St

This enduring spot on the Freedom Trail remains one of the most tangible sites associated with the writers of the New England Renaissance of the last half of the 19th century. Both the *Atlantic Monthly* magazine and Ticknor & Fields (publishers of Ralph Waldo Emerson and Henry David Thoreau) made this modest structure their headquarters during the mid- and late 19th century, when Boston was the literary, intellectual, and publishing center of the country.

Saving the site from demolition in 1960 led to the formation of Historic Boston Incorporated. The building, however, is no longer connected to publishing today.

8 Custom House

MAP Q3 ▪ 3 McKinley Sq
▪ 617 310 6300 ▪ Tours 2pm, 6pm
Sat–Thu ▪ Adm

Custom House clock tower

When the Custom House was built in 1840, Boston was one of America's largest overseas shipping ports, and customs fees were the mainstay of the Federal budget. The Neo-Classical structure once sat on the waterfront, but now stands two blocks inland. The 16-story Custom House tower, added in 1913, was Boston's first skyscraper. Since the 1990s, peregrine falcons have nested in the clock tower under the watchful eyes of wildlife biologists. Tours of the tower gives views of the harbor and the skyline. A bar service is available on evening tours.

9 Post Office Square

MAP Q3

On a sunny day this green oasis in the heart of the Financial District is filled with office workers who claim a bench or a spot of grass for a picnic. Surrounding the park are some of the area's most architecturally distinctive buildings, including the Art Deco post office (Congress St), the Renaissance Revival former Federal Reserve building (now the Langham, Boston hotel, see p146), and the Art Moderne New England Telephone building (185 Franklin St).

Post Office Square at dusk

10 King's Chapel
MAP P3 ■ 58 Tremont St
■ 617 523 1749 ■ Open 10am–5pm
Mon–Sat, 1:30–5pm Sun; call for winter hours; recitals: 12:15pm Tue
■ Adm for tours of crypt and bell tower ■ www.kings-chapel.org

The first Anglican Church in Puritan Boston was established in 1686 to serve British Army officers. When Anglicans fled Boston along with British forces in 1776, the chapel became the first Unitarian Church in the Americas. The church is known for its program of classical concerts.

Interior of King's Chapel

A SHOPPING SPREE

▶ MORNING

The "T" will deposit you at Downtown Crossing, where you can browse the pushcart vendors and shop the fashions and accessories of **Macy's** (450 Washington St) at leisure. Then proceed over to **DSW Shoe Warehouse** (385 Washington St) for a great selection of fashion shoes at discount prices. Make a left up Bromfield Street to peruse the fine writing implements and elegant stationery at **Bromfield Pen Shop** (5 Bromfield St). The walk to Quincy Market down Franklin Street will take you past the Financial District with its tall and imposing skyscrapers. Turn left at **Post Office Square** for lunch at **Sip Café** (Post Office Square Park).

AFTERNOON

Stop to enjoy a short rest outside **Faneuil Hall Marketplace** (see p101) before you begin your spree in earnest. Numerous name-brand shops such as UNIQLO await. For a more local flavor try **Newbury Comics**, which carries a variety of Boston-themed gifts and paraphernalia. Then pay a visit to **Uno de 50** for unusual designs in costume jewelry. Have an early dinner and take in the scene at an outdoor table at **Salty Dog Seafood Grille & Bar** (Quincy Market; 617 742 2094). Order fried seafood, Maine lobster or a complete shore meal. After dinner, rock out to live music at the **Hard Rock Café** (22–24 Clinton St; 617 424 7625).

See map on p100

🔟 Chinatown, the Theater District, and South End

Boston's compact Chinatown is one of the oldest and most significant in the US, concentrating a wealth of Asian experience in a small patch of real estate. Theater-goers find the proximity of Chinatown to the Theater District a boon for pre- and post-show dining. The Theater District itself is among the liveliest in the US, and its architecturally distinctive playhouses are nearly always active, often with local productions. Adjoining the Theater District to the south is South End, once an immigrant tenement area and now Boston's most diverse neighborhood, with strong LGBTQ+ and Latin American

Tremont Street townhouse windows

communities. It is also the country's largest historical district of Victorian townhouses. Following five decades of gentrification and swift inflation of real estate prices, South End is now home to a burgeoning, energetic club, café, and restaurant scene.

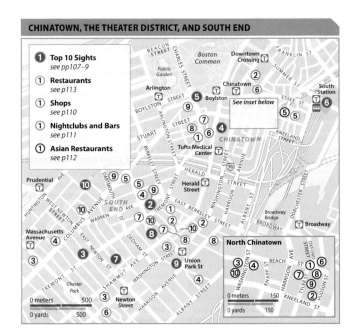

CHINATOWN, THE THEATER DISTRICT, AND SOUTH END

1 **Top 10 Sights**
see pp107–9

1 **Restaurants**
see p113

1 **Shops**
see p110

1 **Nightclubs and Bars**
see p111

1 **Asian Restaurants**
see p112

North Chinatown

0 meters 500
0 yards 500

0 meters 150
0 yards 150

Dragon Gate entrance to Chinatown on Beach Street

1 Beach Street and Chinatown
MAP P5

As the periphery of Chinatown becomes increasingly homogenized, Beach Street remains the purely Chinese heart of the neighborhood. An ornate Dragon Gate at the base of Beach Street creates a ceremonial entrance to Chinatown. Residents also gather to socialize and play cards at the tables located in the small park adjacent to the gate.

2 Boston Center for the Arts
MAP F5 ■ 539 Tremont St ■ 617 426 5000 ■ www.bcaonline.org

The massive Cyclorama building is the centerpiece of the BCA, a performing and visual arts complex dedicated to nurturing new talent. The center (see p54) provides studio space to about 50 artists, and its Mills Gallery mounts rotating visual arts exhibitions. The BCA's four theaters host avant-garde productions of dance, theater, and performance art.

3 Tremont Street
MAP N5–M6

The part of Tremont Street between East Berkeley and Massachusetts Avenue is the social and commercial heart of the South End. Many of the handsome brick and brownstone townhouses have been restored to perfection, some with a boutique or café added at street level. The liveliest corner of the South End is the intersection of Tremont with Clarendon and Union Park streets, where the Boston Center for the Arts and a plethora of restaurants and cafés create a compact entertainment and dining district.

4 Boch Center – Wang Theatre
MAP N5 ■ 270 Tremont St ■ 800 982 2787 ■ www.bochcenter.org

With a theater modeled on the Paris Opera House and a foyer inspired by the Palace of Versailles, the opulent Wang Theatre (see p54), opened in 1925, is a grand venue for touring musicals, blockbuster concerts, and local productions.

Grand foyer of Wang Theatre

Piano Row
MAP N4

During the late 19th century, the headquarters of leading piano makers Steinert, Vose, Starck, Mason & Hamlin, and Wurlitzer were all located on the section of Boylston Street facing Boston Common, giving the block (now a historic district) its nickname of Piano Row. Over a century later, those Beaux Arts buildings still echo with music. The ornate Colonial Theatre opened in 1900. It is owned and managed by Emerson College. Another attraction on Piano Row is Boylston Place, a small-scale club and nightlife center.

South Station
MAP Q5

A temple to mass transportation, the Neo-Classical Revival South Station was erected in 1898 at the height of rail travel in the US, and was once the country's busiest train station. Following extensive restoration in 1989, it now serves as an Amtrak terminal for trains from the south and west of the city, as well as a "T" stop and a social and commercial center with a lively food court and occasional free lunchtime concerts.

Villa Victoria
MAP F6 ■ Area bounded by Shawmut Ave, Tremont St, W Newton St, & W Brookline St ■ Center for the Arts: 85 W Newton St; 617 927 1737; www.ibaboston.org

Villa Victoria is a virtually self-contained, primarily Hispanic neighborhood that grew out of a unique collaboration among Puerto Rican community activists, flexible city planners, and visionary architects. With its low-rise buildings, narrow streets, and mom-and-pop stores, Villa Victoria replicates the feel of Puerto Rican community life. At its heart, the Center for the Arts sponsors concerts and exhibitions. In mid-July the center puts on the Latin American arts and cultural celebration Festival Betances.

Union Park
MAP F6

Constructed between 1857 and 1859, this small park surrounded by English-style brick row houses was built to contrast with the French-inspired grid layout of nearby Back Bay. Graced with lovely trees and fountains and verdant with a thick mat of grass, the square was one of the first areas in the South End to be gentrified.

South Station's imposing Neo-Classical facade

Exterior of Holy Cross Cathedral

⑨ Holy Cross Cathedral
MAP F6 ■ 1400 Washington St ■ 617 542 5682 ■ Open 9am–6pm daily

Holy Cross, the largest Roman Catholic church in Massachusetts, acts as the seat of the archbishop of Boston. The cathedral was constructed between 1866 and 1875 (on the site of the municipal gallows) to serve the largely Irish-American workers who lived in the adjoining shantytown. Today the congregation is principally of Hispanic origin. Of note are the magnificent stained-glass windows, which include rare colored glass imported from Munich in the 19th century, and the powerful Hook & Hastings organ which, when played with the stops out, seems to make every piece of Roxbury pudding-stone in the building reverberate.

⑩ Southwest Corridor Park
MAP E6

The first section of the 5-mile (8-km) Southwest Corridor Park divides South End and Back Bay along the "T" orange line corridor. In the residential South End portion, a path strings together numerous small parks. Between Massachusetts Avenue and West Roxbury, the park broadens to include amenities such as tennis and basketball courts.

EXPLORING CHINATOWN AND SOUTH END

▶ **MORNING**

Begin on Washington Street where you can peruse the exotic produce, Chinese teas, imported Asian spices, and specialty foods at **Jia Ho** (see p110). Continue down Essex Street, ducking into **Oxford Place** to see the mural, *Travelers in an Autumn Landscape*, based on the scroll painting by the same name at the Museum of Fine Arts. The colorful Dragon Gate to **Chinatown** (see p107) stands at the corner of Edinboro Street and Beach Street, along with pagoda-style phone booths. Continue to the corner of Essex and Chauncy where **Essex Corner** (see p110) offers a wide range of goods. Stop for lunch at **Shabu-Zen** (see p112).

AFTERNOON

Walk down **Tremont Street** (see p107) to the South End, or hop on the "T" two stops to Back Bay Station. Head west on Columbus Avenue to see the bronze sculptures that tell the story of freedom seeker Harriet Tubman, who led many enslaved people to freedom on the Underground Railroad, a series of hiding places in free states. Back at Tremont Street, visit the **Boston Center for the Arts** (see p107) to get a snapshot of local contemporary art at the Mills Gallery. Then, if you have time, stroll around the charming **Union Park** before returning to the arts center for dinner and live music at **The Beehive** (see p111). There is a good chance that local jazz artists will be playing.

See map on p106

Shops

1 Jia Ho Supermarket
MAP N5 ▪ 692 Washington St

This compact market offers vegetables, tropical fruits, and packaged foods essential for cuisines from Singapore to Seoul.

2 Flock
MAP P6 ▪ 274 Shawmut Ave
▪ Closed Mon

Flock sells stylish and easy-to-wear women's clothing and accessories with a modern boho flair, plus an eclectic range of gifts and affordable home decor items.

3 Hudson
MAP F6 ▪ 12 Union Park St
▪ Closed Sun & Mon

This home decor boutique offers home furnishings and a delightfully eclectic mix of decorative accent pieces that includes traditional, country, vintage, and modern pieces.

4 Lekker Home
MAP G6 ▪ 38 Wareham St
▪ Closed Mon

Contemporary Italian, Scandinavian, and German home design items are the highlights of this emporium, which offers the latest trends in homeware.

5 Tadpole
MAP M6 ▪ 58 Clarendon St

Tadpole's cheery selection of clothing, toys, and accessories for children are a favorite among the locals. Limited edition strollers are very popular.

Bamboo plants, Essex Corner

6 Essex Corner
MAP P5 ▪ 50 Essex St

This large shop gathers all the Asian merchandise found in Chinatown into one easy-to-peruse location.

7 Michele Mercaldo Jewelry
MAP G6 ▪ 276 Shawmut Ave
▪ Closed Sun–Tue

Jewelry by contemporary designer Michele Mercaldo and her colleagues is displayed in creative and unusual ways at this South End store.

8 Bead & Fiber
MAP G6 ▪ 460 Harrison Ave
▪ Closed Mon

Whether you're looking for beaded jewelry or fiber art, or simply the materials to make them, this shop and gallery offers everything you need, including classes.

9 Urban Grape
MAP L4 ▪ 303 Columbus Ave

This stylish award-winning liquor store uses "progressive shelving", a unique system of organizing wines by their body instead of region or variety to make it easy for customers to select wines.

10 Syrian Grocery Importing Company
MAP G5 ▪ 270 Shawmut Ave
▪ Closed Sun & Mon

Harking back to the South End's days as a Middle Eastern immigrant neighborhood, this grocery sells southern and eastern Mediterranean essentials, from preserved lemons to rare Moroccan argan oil.

Tadpole on Clarendon Street

Nightclubs and Bars

1 Candibar Boston
MAP G5 ■ 275 Tremont St
■ 617 350 8772 ■ Closed Mon–Wed
■ Adm

A melting pot of neon lights, creative cocktails, and glam, futuristic decor, Candibar attracts a diverse crowd.

2 Sip Wine Bar and Kitchen
MAP P5 ■ 581 Washington St

This wine bar serves small plates accompanied by an excellent variety of wines – offered by the bottle or glass.

Sip Wine Bar and Kitchen sign

3 Wally's Café
MAP E6 ■ 427 Massachusetts Ave

Exhale before you squeeze in the door at Wally's. This thin, chock-full sliver of a room is one of the best jazz bars in Boston, and has been since 1944.

4 Five Horses Tavern
MAP F6 ■ 535 Columbus Ave
■ 617 936 3930

This atmospheric, brick-walled tavern boasts an impressive collection of craft beers from around the world. It also serves fine whiskeys and American comfort food.

5 Delux Café
MAP M6 ■ 100 Chandler St
■ Closed Sun

Cheap drinks and an Elvis shrine lend an edge to the trendy scene here. It's good clean fun for hipster grandchildren of the beatniks. Regulars and visitors alike rave about the fried chicken.

6 Royale
MAP P5 ■ 279 Tremont St
■ 617 338 7699 ■ Adm

A massive two-story dance hall, Royale occasionally morphs into a live-performance concert venue for touring acts.

7 Venu
MAP N5 ■ 100 Warrenton St ■ Closed Mon & Wed

Music varies each night of the week, but fashionable and glamorous visitors remain a constant. The Art Deco bar makes for a beautiful look.

8 Jacque's Cabaret
MAP N5 ■ 79 Broadway ■ Adm

A pioneer drag-queen bar, Jacque's features female impersonators, edgy rock bands, and cabaret shows.

9 The Beehive
MAP M6 ■ 541 Tremont St ■ 617 423 0069

Live jazz, delicious cocktails and beers, as well as good, hearty fare make The Beehive one of the best venues in South End.

10 The Butcher Shop
MAP F6 ■ 552 Tremont St

A full-service butcher shop and wine bar pairs sausages, salami, and foie gras terrine with Italian, French, and Spanish wines by the glass or bottle. Gourmet "Burgers and Beers" evenings take place in the summer months.

Interior of The Butcher Shop

See map on p106

Asian Restaurants

1 Peach Farm
MAP P5 ▪ 24 Tyler St
▪ 617 482 3332 ▪ $

Perfect for family-style dining,
the Peach Farm lets you select
your choice of fish from a tank.
Ask for the daily specials.

2 Pho Pasteur
MAP H5 ▪ 682 Washington
St ▪ 617 482 7467 ▪ $

Refreshing Vietnamese noodle
soups flavored with fresh herbs,
top the menu, but other Vietnamese
dishes are also available.

Exterior of Penang

3 Penang
MAP N5 ▪ 685 Washington St
▪ 617 451 6372 ▪ $

Nominally "Pan-Asian," Penang has
a chiefly Malay menu, ranging from
inexpensive noodle staples to more
contemporary concoctions.

4 Emperor's Garden
MAP P5 ▪ 690 Washington St
▪ 617 482 8898 ▪ $

Dim sum in this historical opera
house is a theatrical experience.
Note that most southern Chinese
dishes are large and best shared.

5 Hei La Moon
MAP Q5 ▪ 88 Beach St ▪ 617
338 8813 ▪ $

A huge, rather formal Pan-Chinese
restaurant on the Leather District
side of Atlantic Avenue. On weekend
mornings, a large crowd is guaran-
teed for the dim sum.

6 Taiwan Cafe
MAP P5 ▪ 34 Oxford St ▪ 617
426 8181 ▪ No credit cards ▪ $

From its cafeteria appearance to
its dishes like spicy big ears and
jellyfish, this restaurant delivers
one of the most authentic East Asian
dining experiences in the city.

7 Shojo
MAP P5 ▪ 9A Tyler St ▪ 617
423 7888 ▪ $$

Savor suckling pig *bao* (steamed
stuffed bun) and chicken tacos with
yuzu slaw at this snazzy Japanese
restaurant. Superb craft cocktails.

8 China King
MAP P5 ▪ 60 Beach St ▪ 617
542 1763 ▪ $

This eatery offers an extensive
menu of Chinese delicacies, plus
the must-try Peking duck. Place
your order a day in advance for a
minimum of four diners.

9 Shabu-Zen
MAP P5 ▪ 16 Tyler St ▪ 617
292 8828 ▪ $$

Choose your meats and vegetables
and your cooking liquid at this
traditional Asian "hot-pot" joint.

10 Dumpling Café
MAP G5 ▪ 695 Washington St
▪ 617 338 8858 ▪ $

This casual spot sells several
varieties of dumpling made
fresh daily, alongside delicacies
such as duck tongue.

Diners at Dumpling Café

Restaurants

PRICE CATEGORIES
For a three-course meal for one with half
a bottle of wine (or equivalent meal),
taxes, and extra charges.
....
$ under $40 $$ $40–$60 $$$ over $60

1 B&G Oysters
**MAP F6 ▪ 550 Tremont St
▪ 617 423 0550 ▪ $$$**

A seafood bistro acclaimed for its
raw delicacies, B&G Oysters *(see p65)*
boasts an excellent wine list that per-
fectly complements the dishes.

2 Myers + Chang
**MAP G6 ▪ 1145 Washington St
▪ 617 542 5200 ▪ $$**

Clever reinventions of classic
Chinese dishes such as lemon
shrimp dumplings are served here.
Wash down with sake-based cocktails containing guava and lychee.

3 El Centro
**MAP F6 ▪ 472 Shawmut Ave
▪ 617 262 5708 ▪ $**

Authentic Mexican cuisine from
a Sonoran chef emphasizes fresh
flavors and serves authentic tamales
and tortillas made from scratch.

4 Banyan Bar + Refuge
**MAP F6 ▪ 553 Tremont St
▪ 617 556 4211 ▪ $**

A chic Pan-Asian gastropub, Banyan
Bar + Refuge serves innovative fare
such as roasted chicken with wasabi
gratin potatoes and kimchi fried rice.

5 Troquet on South
**MAP Q5 ▪ 107 South St ▪ 617
695 9463 ▪ Closed Sun & Mon ▪ $$$**

This American–French bistro recom-
mends choosing your wine first and
pairing your food order to its notes.

6 Toro
**MAP F6 ▪ 1704 Washington St
▪ 617 536 4300 ▪ Closed L Sat ▪ $$$**

Enjoy Barcelona-style tapas with
Spanish wines and creative cocktails
at this restaurant.

Aquitaine's classically French interior

7 Aquitaine
**MAP F5 ▪ 569 Tremont St ▪ 617
424 8577 ▪ Closed L Mon–Fri ▪ $$$**

A Parisian-style bistro popular for
its snazzy wine bar and its French
market-style cooking. Black truffle
vinaigrette makes Aquitaine's steak-
frites Boston's best.

8 Franklin Cafe
**MAP F6 ▪ 278 Shawmut Ave
▪ 617 350 0010 ▪ Closed L ▪ $$**

Intimate South End favorite, serving
American bistro fare along with
creative cocktails, local beers, and
affordable wines.

9 Ostra
**MAP N5 ▪ 1 Charles St S
▪ 617 421 1200 ▪ $$$**

This sophisticated restaurant in the
Theater District serves contemporary
Mediterranean fare in both innovative
and classic preparations.

10 Giacomo's
**MAP L6 ▪ 431 Columbus Ave
▪ 617 536 5723 ▪ $**

This offshoot of a very popular North
End eatery offers heaped portions
of filling Italian fare at great prices.
The restaurant accepts cash only.

See map on p106

⬛**10** Kenmore and the Fenway

On days when the Red Sox are playing a home baseball game at Fenway Park, Kenmore Square is packed with fans. By dusk, Kenmore becomes the jump-off point for a night of dancing, drinking, and socializing at clubs on or near Lansdowne Street. Yet for all of Kenmore's genial rowdiness, it is also the gateway into the sedate parkland of the Back Bay Fens and the stately late 19th- and early 20th-century buildings along the Fenway. The Fenway neighborhood extends all the way southeast to Huntington Avenue, also known as the "Avenue of the Arts," which links key cultural centers such as Symphony Hall, Huntington Theatre, the Museum of Fine Arts, Massachusetts College of Art and Design, and the delightful and not-to-be-missed Isabella Stewart Gardner Museum along a tree-lined boulevard.

Entrance to the Back Bay Fens

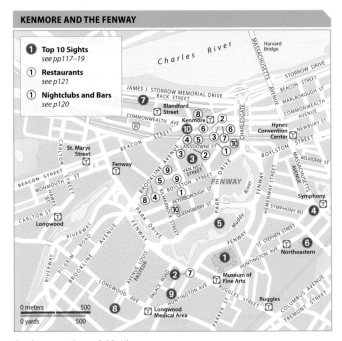

KENMORE AND THE FENWAY

❶ Top 10 Sights
see pp117–19

① Restaurants
see p121

① Nightclubs and Bars
see p120

1 Museum of Fine Arts

One of the largest fine arts museums in the country, the MFA *(see pp28–31)* is especially renowned for its collections of ancient Egyptian and Nubian art and artifacts, as well as of French Impressionism. Its Asian art holdings are said to be the largest in the United States.

2 Isabella Stewart Gardner Museum

This Fenway museum *(see pp34–5)*, in a faux Venetian palace, represents the exquisite personal tastes of its founder, Isabella Stewart Gardner, who was one of the country's premier art collectors at the end of the 19th century.

3 Fenway Park

MAP D5 ▪ 4 Jersey St ▪ 617 226 6666 for tours, 617 267 1700 for tickets ▪ Tours 9am–5pm daily (from 10am in winter; last tour 3 hours before game time) ▪ Adm ▪ www.redsox.com

Built in 1912, the home field of the Boston Red Sox is the oldest surviving park in major league baseball, and aficionados insist that it's also the finest. An odd-shaped parcel of land gives the park quirky features, such as the high, green-painted wall in left field, affectionately known as "the Green Monster." Although previous owners wanted to abandon Fenway, the current ones have enlarged the park to accommodate more loyal Sox fans. Behind-the-scenes tours include areas normally closed to the public, like the dugouts and private boxes.

Performance at Symphony Hall

4 Symphony Hall

MAP E6 ▪ 301 Massachusetts Ave ▪ 617 266 1492 ▪ www.bso.org

The restrained, elegant Italian Renaissance exterior of this 1900 concert hall *(see p54)* barely hints at what is considered to be the acoustic perfection of the interior hall. Home of the Boston Symphony Orchestra, the hall's 2,300-plus seats are usually sold out for their classical concerts, as well as for the lighter Boston Pops.

5 Back Bay Fens

MAP D5–D6 ▪ Bounded by Park Dr & the Fenway

This lush ribbon of grassland, marshes, and stream banks follows Muddy River and forms one link in the Emerald Necklace of parks *(see p19)*. The enclosed James P. Kelleher Rose Garden in the center of the Fens offers a perfect spot for quiet contemplation. A path runs from Kenmore Square to the museums and galleries on Huntington Avenue, which makes a pleasant shortcut through the Fens. Best by daylight.

Panoramic view of the Fenway baseball park

An performance in the magnificent Jordan Hall, NEC

6 Jordan Hall

MAP E6 ▪ 30 Gainsborough St ▪ 617 585 1260 ▪ www.necmusic.edu

This concert hall *(see p55)* is set in the New England Conservatory of Music (NEC). Musicians often praise its acoustics, heralding Jordan as "the Stradivarius of concert halls." Hundreds of free classical concerts are performed at this National Historic Landmark hall every year.

A play at Boston Playwrights' Theatre

7 Boston University

Howard Gotlieb Archival Research Center: MAP C4; 771 Commonwealth Ave; 617 353 3696; exhibit rooms open 9am–4pm Mon–Fri; adm ▪ Boston Playwrights' Theatre: MAP C5; 949 Commonwealth Ave; 866 811 4111; season runs Oct–Apr ▪ www.bu.edu

Founded as a Methodist Seminary in 1839, Boston University was chartered as a university in 1869. Today it enrolls approximately 34,000 students from all 50 states and some 125 countries. The scattered colleges and schools were consolidated at the Charles River Campus in 1966. Both sides of Commonwealth Avenue are lined with distinctive university buildings and sculptures. The Howard Gotlieb Archival Research Center lays emphasis on the memorabilia of show business figures, displayed on a rotating basis. Artifacts include Gene Kelly's Oscar and a number of Bette Davis's film scripts. It also exhibits selections from its holdings of rare manuscripts and books. The Boston Playwrights' Theatre was founded by the late Nobel Laureate Derek Walcott in 1981 to help develop new plays. A season highlight is the day-long Boston Theater Marathon of 50 ten-minute plays.

8 Warren Anatomical Museum

MAP C6 ▪ 10 Shattuck St ▪ 617 432 2136 ▪ Open 9am–5pm Mon–Fri

Established in 1847 from the private holdings of Dr. John Collins Warren, this museum contains the former anatomical teaching collections of the Harvard Medical School, including clinical examples of rare deformities and diseases. Among the excellent displays are several delicate and poignant skeletons of stillborn conjoined twins. The unusual collections are still used for medical education.

9 Massachusetts College of Art and Design Museum

MAP D6 ■ 621 Huntington Ave ■ 617 879 7337 ■ Call in advance for opening hours ■ www.massart.edu

Opened in early 2020 after extensive renovation, the MassArt Museum set in the school's South Building mounts some of Boston's most dynamic exhibitions of contemporary visual art. It is the only independent state-supported art college in the US and exhibitions tend to emphasize avant-garde experimentation as well as social commentary and documentary.

10 Kenmore Square

MAP D5

Largely dominated by Boston University, Kenmore Square is now being transformed from a student ghetto into an extension of upmarket Back Bay, losing some of its funky character but gaining élan in the process. As the public transportation gateway to Fenway Park, the square swarms with baseball fans and sidewalk vendors, rather than students, on game days. The most prominent landmark of the square is the CITGO sign, its more than 9,000 ft (2,743 m) of LEDs pulsing red, white, and blue from dusk until midnight. *Time* magazine designated this sign an "objet d'heart" because it was so beloved by Bostonians that they prevented its dismantling in 1983.

Kenmore Square, with its CITGO sign

See map on p116

A DAY OF THE ARTS

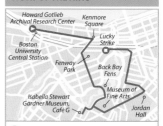

► MORNING AND AFTERNOON

Take the green line "T" (B train) to Boston University Central and make your way to the Howard Gotlieb Archival Research Center, part of **Boston University**, for a glimpse of show business ephemera, such as Fred Astaire's dance shoes. Then head east toward **Kenmore Square** and cross over to Brookline Avenue in front of **Hotel Commonwealth** *(see p148)*. Stroll along Brookline Avenue, on to **Fenway Park** *(see p117)* for a tour of America's most beloved baseball stadium and then take Jersey Street to the **Back Bay Fens** *(see p117)*, where you can rest beneath the wings of the angel on the Veteran's Memorial. Continue to the **Museum of Fine Arts** *(see p117)* to view the outstanding art collections – from ancient Egyptian artifacts to contemporary installations. Afterward, follow the Fenway three blocks left to continue your immersion in art at the **Isabella Stewart Gardner Museum** *(see p117)*. Take a break in the "living room" of the museum's Renzo Piano-designed wing, then grab a seat and have a bite to eat at the classy **Café G** *(see p121)*.

EVENING

You can pack in a full evening of entertainment by taking in a recital at **Jordan Hall**. When the final applause has died down, make your way to **Lucky Strike** *(see p120)* and round off the night with billiards, bowling, and video games. You may want to continue into the early hours.

Nightclubs and Bars

1 **Loretta's Last Call**
MAP D5 ▪ 1 Lansdowne St

Country music and Southern food fuel this happening bar and dance club. The interior has a cozy, vintage ambience.

2 **Bleacher Bar**
MAP D5 ▪ 82A Lansdowne St

This tiny bar, tucked in the back of Fenway Park, has several seats offering direct views into the venue. Inviting pub fare and a well-stocked bar keep customers occupied.

3 **Audubon Boston**
MAP D5 ▪ 836 Beacon St

Close enough to Fenway Park to drop by after the game, Audubon Boston is a relaxed neighborhood bar and grill with good food, beer, and a thoughtful wine list.

4 **Cask 'n Flagon**
MAP D5 ▪ 62 Brookline Ave
▪ Closed Sun

At Fenway's premier sports bar, fans hoist a cold one and debate the merits of the Sox manager's latest tactics.

5 **House of Blues**
MAP D5 ▪ 15 Lansdowne St
▪ 888 693 2583 ▪ Adm

An integral part of the nightlife scene around Fenway Park, the House of Blues (see p56) hosts local as well as international bands and performers.

Game On! sports bar

A Gospel brunch is offered occasionally and the restaurant opens during Red Sox evening home games.

6 **Game On!**
MAP D5 ▪ 82 Lansdowne St

Wall-to-wall TVs are tuned to every game that's on anywhere in the country at this bar in a corner of Fenway Park. A prime spot for sports fans to eat, drink, and cheer.

7 **The Kenmore**
MAP D5
▪ 475 Commonwealth Ave

Craft beers, burgers, hot dogs, and nachos make The Kenmore the perfect college hangout bar.

8 **Cornwall's Pub**
MAP D5 ▪ 654 Beacon St

Offering the very best of both worlds, Cornwall's is a British-style pub with a wide range of good beers, ales, and food, but the bartenders also understand baseball.

9 **Yard House**
MAP D5 ▪ 126 Brookline St

Yard House offers more than 100 beers, from local brewers and beyond. It also serves excellent pub food. Calorie count disclosures are listed on the menu.

10 **Lucky Strike**
MAP D5 ▪ 145 Ipswich St

Set behind Fenway Park, this entertainment complex features bowling lanes, pool tables, and video games, as well as the popular brewpub, Cheeky Monkey.

House of Blues near Fenway Park

Restaurants

1 Citizen Public House
MAP E5 ▪ 1310 Boylston St
▪ 617 450 9000 ▪ $$
Craft beers, 100 whiskeys, excellent cocktails, and great pub food make Citizen a top neighborhood spot.

2 Eventide Fenway
MAP D5 ▪ 51321 Boylston St
▪ 617 545 1060 ▪ Closed Mon–Tue, L Wed–Fri ▪ $$
Crowds congregate here to dine on freshly shucked oysters, brown butter lobster rolls, and, for dessert, whoopie pies.

3 India Quality
MAP D4 ▪ 484 Commonwealth Ave ▪ 617 267 4499 ▪ $
Long-time favorite of Boston University students, India Quality focuses on north Indian food roasted in a tandoor oven. It serves several excellent fish dishes and spicy plates as well.

Simple interior of Sweet Cheeks Q

4 Sweet Cheeks Q
MAP E5 ▪ 1381 Boylston St
▪ 617 266 1300 ▪ $$
Chef-owner Tiffani Faison is crazy about authentic Southern barbecue. Order pork belly by the pound and drink sweet tea from Mason jars.

PRICE CATEGORIES
For a three-course meal for one with half a bottle of wine (or equivalent meal), taxes and extra charges.

$ under $40 $$ $40–$60 $$$ over $60

5 Wahlburgers
MAP D5 ▪ 132 Brookline Ave
▪ 617 927 6810 ▪ $
Chef Paul, brother of actor Mark Walhberg, runs this casual restaurant that serves burgers with a twist.

6 Tsurutontan Udon Noodle Brasserie
MAP D5 ▪ 512 Commonwealth Ave ▪ 857 233 2839 ▪ $$
Udon noodle bowls and sushi may be the highlights of the menu, but look out for indulgent Japanese treats such as creamy uni with caviar.

7 Café G
MAP D6 ▪ 25 Evans Way
▪ 617 566 1088 ▪ Closed D, Mon ▪ $
Superb light fare, rich desserts, and fine wines at this spot complete a visit to the Isabella Stewart Gardner Museum (see pp34–5).

8 Nathálie Wine Bar
MAP D5 ▪ 186 Brookline Ave ▪ 857 317 3884 ▪ $$
Dishes such as flatiron steak, seared octopus, and fried mushrooms in tomato yogurt are accompanied by a great wine list here.

9 Tasty Burger
MAP D5 ▪ 1301 Boylston St
▪ 617 425 4444 ▪ $
This no-frills burger joint in the shadow of Fenway Park offers a variety of toppings and a wide assortment of beer.

10 El Pelon Taqueria
MAP D5 ▪ 92 Peterborough St
▪ 617 262 9090 ▪ $
A charming little restaurant that churns out tasty Mexican American treats at very competitive prices.

See map on p116 ←

⑩ Cambridge and Somerville

Harvard may be Cambridge's undeniable claim to worldwide fame, but that is not to diminish the city's vibrant neighborhoods, superb restaurants, unique shops, and colorful bars lying just beyond the school's gates. Harvard Square, with its name-brand shopping and numerous coffeehouses, is a heady mix of urban bohemia and Main Street USA. To the northwest, the heavily residential city of Somerville has become a magnet for young artists, musicians, and social media practitioners. Quirky shops and bars fill its squares.

Exhibit at Peabody Museum

CAMBRIDGE AND SOMERVILLE

1 Harvard University

While its stellar reputation might suggest visions of ivory towers in the sky, Harvard *(see pp20–23)* is a surprisingly accessible, welcoming place. Still, too often, visitors limit themselves to what is visible from the Yard: Massachusetts Hall, the Widener Library, maybe University Hall. But with other buildings by Gropius and Le Corbusier, top-notch museums, the eclectic Harvard Square, and performing arts spaces such as the Loeb Drama Center and Memorial Hall's Sanders Theatre *(see p55)* lying just beyond the Yard, Harvard provides every incentive to linger a while.

2 Harvard Art Museums

MAP B1 ▪ 32 Quincy St ▪ 617 495 9400 ▪ Open 10am–5pm daily ▪ Adm ▪ www.harvard artmuseums.org

Harvard has some of the world's finest collegiate art collections. The Fogg, Sackler, and Busch-Reisinger museums, which make up the Harvard Art Museums *(see p21)*, share space in a Renzo Piano-designed facility. Visitors will enjoy the surprising juxtapositions of Chinese bronzes, Greek vases, medieval altarpieces, and German Expressionist paintings with a visit to all three museums.

The Museum of Natural History

3 Harvard Museums of Science & Culture

Peabody Museum: MAP B1; 11 Divinity Ave; 617 496 1027; open 9am–5pm daily; adm ▪ Museum of Natural History: MAP B1; 26 Oxford St; 617 495 3045; open 9am–5pm daily; adm ▪ www.hmsc.harvard.edu

Its ongoing commitment to research aside, the Peabody Museum of Archaeology & Ethnology *(see p21)* excels at illustrating how interactions between distinct cultures influence peoples' lives. The Hall of the North American Indian displays artifacts reflecting the aftermath of encounters between Native Americans and Europeans. The Museum of Natural History *(see p20)* has exhibits that display eons-old natural wonders.

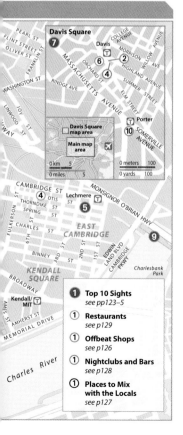

4 Charles Riverbanks
MAP B2–F3

Whether you're cheering the rowers of the Head of the Charles Regatta (see p73) or watching the "T" cross Longfellow Bridge through a barrage of snowflakes, the banks (see p127) of the Charles River offer a fantastic vantage point for taking in Boston's celebrated scenes. On summer Sundays, the adjacent Memorial Drive becomes a sea of strollers, joggers, and rollerbladers.

5 Multicultural Arts Center
MAP F2 ▪ 41 2nd St ▪ 617 577 1400 ▪ Open 10:30am–6pm Mon–Fri

Housed in a beautiful 19th-century courthouse, the MAC presents a range of performance and visual art exhibitions which promote cross-cultural exchange, including summer programs in local parks. A unique feature is the encouragement of dialogue between audience and artists after performances and openings.

Multicultural Arts Center

6 Inman Square
MAP D1

Often overlooked, Inman Square is possibly Cambridge's best-kept secret. Home to popular restaurants and cafés such as S&S Deli, 1369 Coffee House (see p127), and Trina's Starlight Lounge, plus Christina's delectable ice creams (see p67), Inman rewards those who are willing to go out of their way to experience a real-deal Cambridge neighborhood.

Somerville Theatre, Davis Square

7 Davis Square
With its cooler-than-thou coffee shops, lively bar scene, affordable restaurants, and the renowned Somerville Theatre (see p54), Davis Square, Somerville, stands as the area's most desirable neighborhood for many young Bostonians. And with prestigious Tufts University a 10-minute walk away, the square's youthful spirit is in a constant state of replenishment.

8 Longfellow House
▪ MAP A1 ▪ 105 Brattle St ▪ 617 876 4491 ▪ Open Jun–Oct: 9:30am–5pm Wed–Sun for tours only ▪ www.nps.gov/long

Poet Henry Wadsworth Longfellow can be credited with helping to shape Boston's – and America's – collective identity. His poetic documentation of Paul Revere's midnight ride (see p44) immortalized both him and his subject. In 1837, Longfellow took up residence in this house, a few blocks from Harvard Yard. He was not the first illustrious resident of this house. General George Washington headquartered

---

LOCAL STAGES

The performing arts form part of the character of Cambridge and Somerville. The ornate Somerville Theatre (see p54) draws nationally recognized musical acts, while the Loeb Drama Center (64 Brattle St; 617 547 8300) stages The American Repertory Theater's daring, top-notch productions. And Harvard student-produced pieces grace the Hasty Pudding Theater's stage (12 Holyoke St, Cambridge; 617 495 5205).

and planned the 1776 siege of Boston in these rooms. The building is preserved with furnishings of Longfellow's family life, and houses the poet's archives.

9 Museum of Science

MAP N1 ■ Science Park ■ 617 723 2500 ■ Open 9am–5pm Mon–Thu, Sat & Sun, 9am–9pm Fri ■ Adm ■ www.mos.org

Explore the cosmos in the Hayden Planetarium, admire a full-size model of a T-Rex, and experience larger-than-life IMAX® films in the Mugar Omni Theater – the Museum of Science certainly knows how to make learning enjoyable. In addition to these attractions, the museum hosts blockbuster shows like Harry Potter: The Exhibit. Live presentations take place throughout the day.

Massachusetts Institute of Technology

10 Massachusetts Institute of Technology (MIT)

MAP D3 ■ 77 Massachusetts Ave ■ 617 253 4795 ■ List Visual Arts Center: 20 Ames St, Cambridge; 617 253 4680; open noon–6pm Tue–Sun (to 8pm Thu) ■ MIT Museum: 314 Main St; 617 253 5927; open 10am–5pm daily (to 6pm Jul–Aug); adm ■ www.mit.edu

MIT has been the country's leading technical university since its founding in 1861. Its List Visual Arts Center exhibits work that comments on technology or employs it in fresh, surprising ways. Also of note is the MIT Museum, with its interactive exhibits on such fascinating topics as artificial intelligence, holography, and the world's first computers.

THE CAMBRIDGE CURRICULUM

▶ MORNING

Begin your morning with a cup of gourmet coffee and light breakfast at the popular **Diesel Café** *(see p58)* on **Davis Square**. Next, ride the "T" inbound to Harvard and head straight to the independent **Harvard Bookstore** *(1256 Massachusetts Ave)* to peruse its expertly curated selection of titles. Visit **Harvard Yard** *(see p20)* and the John Harvard Statue and then walk east to Quincy Street and north to the **Harvard Art Museums** *(see p123)*. Walk south to Massachusetts Avenue, and turn right to legendary **Mr Bartley's** *(1246 Massachusetts Ave)* for a lunch of specialty burgers and sweet potato fries.

AFTERNOON

Ride the "T" inbound to Central Square, and walk southeast along Massachusetts Avenue to the **MIT Museum**, where exhibits of scientific, artistic and technological innovations reflect the creative energy of MIT. Return to Central Square and ride the "T" to Park Street. Then ride the Green Line "T" to Science Park and the **Museum of Science**. In this museum you can choose from 700 interactive exhibits, view classic dioramas of New England landscapes, learn about nanotechnology, and explore the biology of human life. Then retrace your route on the "T" to Central Square, where you can sit back and enjoy a refreshing glass of hard cider on the patio at **The Station** *(438 Massachusetts Ave)*.

See map on pp122–3

Offbeat Shops

① Top Drawer
MAP B1
- 5 Brattle St, Cambridge

From beautiful pens to Japanese handkerchiefs, this is the perfect place to pick up a gift.

② Magpie
416 Highland Ave, Somerville

This Davis Square boutique is packed with handmade art and crafts by local artists, goods from indie designers, and "shiny things for your nest."

③ Ward Maps
1735 Massachusetts Ave, Cambridge
- Closed Mon

In addition to some utterly lovely antique map reproductions, this shop stocks MBTA-themed items such as mugs, key chains, tote bags, as well as toy trains, and buses.

④ Motto
26 Church St, Cambridge
- Closed Sun

A stylish shop selling women's clothing, jewelry, and accessories designed by up-and-coming names. Motto also stocks stylish homeware, including Japanese ceramics.

⑤ Hubba Hubba
MAP C2 - 2 Ellery St, Cambridge - Closed Sun

If Cambridge's Puritanical founders could see it now – spiked belts,

Window display, Hubba Hubba

accessories, leather corsets, and adult toys line the shelves of this risqué boutique.

⑥ The Million Year Picnic
MAP A1 - 99 Mt Auburn St, Cambridge

New England's oldest comic bookstore, The Million Year Picnic keeps its faithful customers happy with an extensive back-issue selection, graphic novels, rare imports, and all the latest indie comics, along with toys and T-shirts.

Vintage comics, The Million Year Picnic

⑦ NOMAD
1771 Massachusetts Ave, Cambridge

Clothing, folk art, and decor items from around the globe are among the wares for sale here. There is a visibly strong emphasis on goods from Mexico and Central America at NOMAD.

⑧ Davis Squared
409 Highland Ave #2516, Somerville - Closed Mon & Tue

This fun shop abounds with Davis Square- and Somerville-themed goods, ranging from coffee mugs to wine decanters.

⑨ Cardullo's Gourmet Shoppe
MAP B1 - 6 Brattle St, Cambridge

Harvard Square's oldest culinary store specializes in gourmet foods and beverages from around the world. You can also buy made-to-order deli sandwiches for lunch.

⑩ Porter Exchange Mall
1815 Massachusetts Ave, Cambridge

Set in a 1928 renovated Art Deco building, this mall houses a Japanese-style noodle hall and a gift shop with all sorts of wonderful Far Eastern ephemera.

Places to Mix with the Locals

Memorial Drive in the fall

1 Memorial Drive
MAP B4–F3

Memorial Drive is a magnet for joggers and rollerbladers. On summer Sundays, the road closes to vehicular traffic and becomes the city's best people-watching spot.

2 The Pit
MAP B1 ■ Bounded by JFK St & Massachusetts Ave, Cambridge

On and around this sunken brick platform, street musicians, protesters, punk rockers, and uncategorizables create a scene worthy of a *Life* magazine spread.

3 The Neighborhood
MAP D1 ■ 25 Bow St, Somerville ■ 617 623 9710 ■ $

Sunday brunch at the Neighborhood brings throngs intent on securing seating beneath the outdoor grape arbors. Equally coveted are the Portuguese breakfast bread platters.

4 1369 Coffee House
MAP D1 ■ 1369 Cambridge St, Cambridge ■ 617 576 1369 ■ $

Set on Inman Square, this branch of 1369 has poetry readings, mellow music, and courteous staff, which give it a neighborly atmosphere.

5 Brattle Theatre
MAP B1 ■ 40 Brattle St, Cambridge ■ 617 876 6837

A Harvard Square institution, the Brattle screens cinema greats daily. Visiting on a rainy afternoon? Take in a 2-for-1 Fellini double feature for under $15.

6 Cambridge Public Library
MAP C2 ■ 449 Broadway, Cambridge ■ 617 349 4040

Families with children, dog-owners tending to canine playgroups, and locals cover the lawns in warm weather. Indoors, folks stretch out in armchairs with a book and free Wi-Fi.

7 Fresh Pond Reservation
250 Fresh Pond Pkwy, Cambridge ■ 617 349 4770

Join Cambridge's runners and dog-walkers on the 2.5-mile (4-km) loop trail around Fresh Pond. Along the way, look out for waterfowl and owls.

8 Club Passim
MAP B1 ■ 47 Palmer St, Cambridge ■ 617 492 7679

The subterranean epicenter of New England's thriving folk music scene regularly welcomes nationally renowned artists. It also has an on-site restaurant, The Kitchen, which serves dinner and Sunday brunch.

9 Trum Field
Broadway, Somerville

Summer in Somerville is epitomized by one thing – baseball at the playground. On most weeknights, you can watch energetic youngsters take their swings.

10 Dado Tea
MAP B1 ■ 955 Massachusetts Ave, Cambridge ■ 617 497 9061

This Massachusetts Avenue hangout, owned by locals, is a serene, tranquil place to settle in with a cup of exotic tea and healthy pastries, sandwiches, wraps, and salads.

See map on pp122–3

Nightclubs and Bars

The Middle East live music club

1 The Middle East
MAP D3 ▪ 472–480 Massachusetts Ave, Cambridge ▪ 617 864 3278 ▪ Adm

A live music club to rival any in New York or Los Angeles, the Middle East rocks its patrons from three stages and nourishes them with delicious kebabs and curries.

2 Sinclair
MAP B1 ▪ 52 Church St

Harvard Square's primary live gig venue attracts a wide assortment of acts. The front room doubles as a trendy restaurant and lounge, and it's open into the small hours every night of the week.

3 Regattabar
MAP B2 ▪ 1 Bennett St, Cambridge ▪ Closed Sun & Mon

Befitting its location in the sleek Charles Hotel, Regattabar offers a refined yet casual setting for watching jazz giants. Shows sell out quickly.

4 The Burren
247 Elm St, Somerville ▪ 617 776 6896

This friendly Irish bar features live music almost every night, and the performances range from Irish sessions to bluegrass to swing and jazz. The backroom has comedy, step-dancing, and a weekly open mic.

5 Backbar
MAP D1 ▪ 7 Sanborn Ct, Somerville ▪ 617 249 3522

Somerville-Cambridge hipsters love this bar because of its gritty location, speakeasy vibe, and world-class cocktails.

6 Hong Kong
MAP B2 ▪ 1238 Massachusetts Ave, Cambridge ▪ Comedy club closed Mon

Chinese food at ground level gives way to a bustling lounge on the second floor and a raucous comedy nightclub on the third. Tuesday night features a comic magic show.

7 Lord Hobo
MAP D2 ▪ 292 Hampshire St, Cambridge

Forty draft beers, homey bistro food, and an inventive cocktail program draw an eclectic crowd, from hipsters to software geeks.

8 Lizard Lounge
MAP B1 ▪ 1667 Massachusetts Ave, Cambridge

Just outside Harvard Square, the Lizard Lounge attracts a young, alternative rock- and folk-loving crowd with the promise of good live music and a small cover charge.

9 The Cantab Lounge
MAP C2 ▪ 738 Massachusetts Ave, Cambridge

Live local rock performances, poetry slams, open mic nights, and other such events light up the small but energetic stage at this blue-collar beer bar in Central Square.

10 Beat Brew Hall
MAP B1 ▪ 13 Brattle St, Cambridge

Beat is a modern beer hall that serves over 24 beers on draft, craft cocktails, and delicious pub fare in a convivial setting. The bar features communal tables and live music.

Restaurants

1 Oleana
MAP D2 ■ 134 Hampshire St, Cambridge ■ 617 661 0505 ■ Closed L daily ■ $$$

Chef Ana Sortun's mastery of spices is evident in Oleana's sumptuous Middle Eastern cuisine (see p62), served in an elegant dining room and a pretty courtyard with a fountain.

2 Pammy's
MAP C2 ■ 928 Massachusetts Ave, Cambridge ■ 617 945 1761 ■ $$$

Flavors of New American cuisine are combined with Italian tradition to create delicious plates at Pammy's (see p62).

Grilled shrimp with bucatini at Pammy's

3 Craigie On Main
MAP D3 ■ 853 Main St, Cambridge ■ 617 497 5511 ■ $$$

"Nose-to-tail" fine dining is the style at Tony Maw's main venue. The menu changes daily, and includes six- and eight-course tasting versions.

4 Courthouse Seafood
MAP E2 ■ 498 Cambridge St, Cambridge ■ 617 491 1213 ■ Closed Sun & Mon ■ $

Adjoining a fish market, this no-frills restaurant is run by a Portuguese family. They always use the freshest catch in their food.

5 Catalyst
MAP E3 ■ 300 Technology Sq, Cambridge ■ 617 576 3000 ■ $$

This elegant restaurant serves innovative locavore dishes. Craft beers attract the coders while good wines soothe the biotech execs. Its summer patio is a real plus.

6 Redbones
55 Chester St, Somerville ■ 617 628 2200 ■ $$

Redbones' kitchen creates some of the best barbecue north of the Carolinas, and the atmosphere is emphatically Southern.

7 Viale
MAP C3 ■ 502 Massachusetts Ave, Cambridge ■ 617 576 1900 ■ Closed L daily ■ $$$

Delightful Mediterranean dishes and innovative cocktails make this friendly bar-restaurant a go-to place for food and drinks.

8 Area 4
MAP D2 ■ 500 Technology Sq, Cambridge ■ 617 758 4444 ■ $

Service begins as early as 7am at this bakery-café, and continues into the night with New American comfort food and pizzas.

9 Puritan & Company
MAP D2 ■ 1166 Cambridge St, Cambridge ■ 617 876 0286 ■ Closed L Mon–Sat ■ $$$

Excellent farm-to-table dining venue that re-invents New England cuisine with dishes such as seared scallops with tomatillos. Sunday brunch is a major foodie scene.

10 Harvest
MAP B1 ■ 44 Brattle St, Cambridge ■ 617 868 2255 ■ $$$

A local institution, Harvest (see p63) serves delicious contemporary dishes, all prepared with fresh seasonal ingredients. The restaurant is known for its superb three-course Sunday brunch.

See map on pp122–3

🔟 South of Boston

South of Fort Point Channel, Boston's neighborhoods of Jamaica Plain, Roxbury, Dorchester, and South Boston are a mixture of densely residential streets and leafy parklands that form part of Frederick Law Olmsted's Emerald Necklace. The lively street scenes of Boston's African American, Latin American, and Irish American communities make the city's southerly neighborhoods a dynamic contrast to the more homogenized city core. Often ignored by tourists, the area south of Boston is full of quirky shops, local bars, hot nightclubs, and great places to enjoy dishes from many of the city's minority communities. This area is a little harder to reach but it is worth the effort to experience a more diverse Boston.

Forest Hills Cemetery in Fall

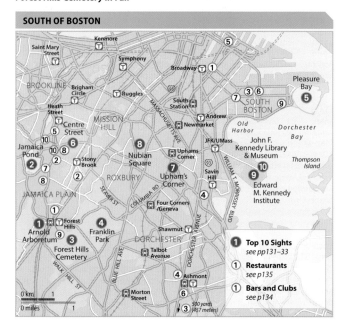

SOUTH OF BOSTON

Top 10 Sights
see pp131–33

Restaurants
see p135

Bars and Clubs
see p134

The lush green Arnold Arboretum

① Arnold Arboretum
125 Arborway, Jamaica Plain
■ **617 524 1718**

One of the US's foremost collections of temperate-zone trees and shrubs covers the peaceful 0.4-sq-mile- (1.1-sq-km-) arboretum. Grouped in scientific fashion, they are a favorite subject for landscape painters, and a popular resource for botanists and gardeners. The world's most extensive lilac collection blooms from early May through late June, and thousands of Bostonians turn out for Lilac Sunday, in mid-May, to picnic and enjoy the peak of the Syringa blooms. The main flowering period of mountain laurel, azaleas, and other rhododendrons begins around Memorial Day (at the end of May).

② Jamaica Pond
Jamaica Pond Boathouse, Jamaica Way ■ **617 522 5061** ■ **Open May–Oct: noon–sunset Mon–Thu, 10am–sunset Fri–Sun** ■ **www.boston. gov/parks/jamaica-pond**

This appealing large pond and its surrounding leafy park was land-scaped by Frederick Law Olmsted to accentuate its natural glacial features and it offers an enchanting piece of countryside within the city. Locals enjoy the 1.5-mile (2.5-km) bankside path or fish in the 53-ft- (16-m-) deep glacial kettle pond (fishing requires a Massachusetts license, call 617626 1590). The boat-house rents small sailboats, kayaks, and rowboats in summer.

③ Forest Hills Cemetery
95 Forest Hills Ave, Jamaica Plain ■ **617 524 0128**

More than 100,000 graves dot the rolling landscape in this Victorian "garden cemetery," one of the first of its kind. Maps available at the entrance identify the graves of notable figures, such as poet E. E. Cummings and play-wright Eugene O'Neill. Striking memorials include the bas-relief *Death Stays the Hand of the Artist* by Daniel Chester French, near wthe main entrance.

④ Franklin Park
Franklin Park Rd, Dorchester ■ **617 265 4084**

Frederick Law Olmsted considered Franklin Park the masterpiece of his Emerald Necklace *(see p19)*, but his vision of urban wilds has since been modified to more modern uses. The park is home to the second-oldest municipal golf course in the US and the child-friendly Franklin Park Zoo *(see p53)*, which contrasts contemporary ecological exhibits with charming zoo architecture, such as a 1913 *pagoda*-style bird house.

A playground at Franklin Park Zoo

The tranquil beach at Pleasure Bay

5 Pleasure Bay

South Boston's Pleasure Bay park encloses a pond-like cove of Boston Harbor with a causeway boardwalk, where locals turn out for their daily constitutionals. Castle Island, now attached to the mainland, has guarded the mouth of Boston Harbor since the first fortress was erected in 1634. As New England's oldest continually fortified site, it is now guarded by Fort Independence (c. 1851). Anglers gather on the adjacent Steel Pier and drop bait into the mass of striped bass and bluefish.

6 Centre Street

Jamaica Plain is home to many artists, musicians, and writers as well as a substantial portion of Boston's LGBTQ+ community. Centre Street is the main artery and hub. There is a distinctly Latin American flavor at the Jackson Square end, where Caribbean music shops and

Centre Street, Jamaica Plain

Cuban, Dominican, and Mexican eateries abound. At the 600 block, Centre Street morphs into an urban counter-cultural village, with design boutiques, funky second-hand stores, and small cafés and restaurants.

7 Upham's Corner

Strand Theatre, 543 Columbia Rd, Dorchester ▪ 617 635 1403

The area known as Upham's Corner was founded in 1630, and its venerable Old Dorchester Burial Ground contains ethereal carved stones from this Puritan era. Today, Upham's Corner is decidedly more Caribbean than Puritan, with shops specializing in food, clothing, and the music of the islands. The Strand Theatre, a 1918 luxury movie palace and vaudeville hall, functions as an arts center and venue for live concerts and religious revival meetings.

8 Nubian Square

Dillaway-Thomas House: 183 Roxbury St, Roxbury; 617 445 3399; call in advance for tour hours

Roxbury's Nubian Square is the heart of African American Boston as well as the busiest hub in the city's public transportation network. The Beaux Arts station is modeled on the great train stations of Europe. A few blocks from the square, the modest Georgian-style Dillaway-Thomas House reveals Roxbury's early history, including the period when it served as headquarters for the Continental

Army's General John Thomas during the Siege of Boston. Exhibits at the house reflect the area's history from the Colonial era to the present as a center of African American culture in Boston.

⑨ Edward M. Kennedy Institute for the United States Senate

210 Morrissey Blvd, Dorchester ▪ 617 740 7000 ▪ 10am–5pm Tue– Sun ▪ Adm ▪ www.emkinstitute.org

Displaying re-creations of the US Senate Chamber and Senator Edward M. Kennedy's office, this facility provides an impressive interactive experience of how the Senate functions. With film and live actors, "Great Senate Debates" re-creates historic turning points in the Senate.

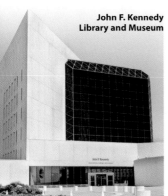

John F. Kennedy Library and Museum

⑩ John F. Kennedy Library and Museum

Columbia Point, Dorchester ▪ 617 514 1600 ▪ Open 9am–5pm daily ▪ Adm ▪ www.jfklibrary.org

This nine-story pyramidal building designed by I. M. Pei in 1977 stands like a billowing sail on Columbia Point. Inside, exhibits recount the 1,000 days of the Kennedy presidency. Kennedy was the first president to grasp the power of broadcast, and video exhibits include campaign debates, as well as coverage of his assassination and funeral.

STREET HEAT & POND COOL IN JAMAICA PLAIN

▶ AFTERNOON

The Orange Line "T" delivers you to the Latin American end of Jamaica Plain's **Centre Street** at Jackson Square, where life is more Santo Domingo than "Downtown Boston". Head west and ease into the rhythm by sampling empanadas, coffee, and Latin American desserts at 🍴 Gondres Bakery *(333 Centre St)*. A walk along Centre Street serves a cornucopia of Latin American fashion and specialty shops. Follow Centre Street as it doglegs left. Hip **Streetcar** *(488 Centre St)* carries a large selection of boutique wines and craft beers. At **J P Licks** *(659 Centre St)* order a cone of super-premium ice cream, and continue to **Boing! JP's Toy Shop** *(667 Centre St)* to discover fun gifts for kids of all ages. **Kitchenwitch** *(671 Centre St)* features all kinds of kitchenware including bamboo salt boxes and silicon handles for cast-iron skillets. Jeweler Phil Celeste carries unique clothing, jewelry and gift items at **On Centre** *(676 Centre St)*. The thrift store **Boomerangs** *(716 Centre St)* has clothing and home decor. **Salmagundi** *(765 Centre St)* is the place to go for hat shopping. Stroll up Burroughs Street and cross Jamaicaway to **Jamaica Pond** *(see p131)* to stroll, sit in the shade, or rent a rowboat.

EVENING

Work up an appetite and return to Centre Street for dinner at 🍽 Vee Vee *(see p135)*. Afterward, hit ultra-hip **Midway Cafe** *(see p134)* 🍺 for a chilled beer and live music.

See map on p130 ←

Bars and Clubs

1 The Jeannie Johnston
144 South St, Jamaica Plain

This entertainment venue has plenty to offer, with an open mic on Thursdays, live local bands on Fridays, and karaoke on Saturdays. There is a snug spot to sit with one of its 35 draft or bottled beers.

2 Midway Cafe
3496 Washington St, Jamaica Plain

A fixture on the Boston live music scene since 1987, Midway hosts every kind of band imaginable. The highlight of the weekly calendar is Thursday night's "Queeraoke".

3 The Playwright Bar
658 East Broadway, South Boston

A stylish Irish punk pub, serving good bar-friendly food (including burgers, wings, and fish and chips) and a range of local and non-local beers.

4 dbar
1236 Dorchester Ave, Dorchester

The eclectic dinner menu disappears around 10pm, when dbar morphs into a hopping, diverse nightclub where brightly colored cocktails are a specialty. Enjoy show tunes on Tuesdays, karaoke on Fridays.

5 Lucky's Lounge
355 Congress St, South Boston

A Fort Point Channel underground bar that swaggers with rat-pack retro ambience, right down to the lounge acts and the unmissable Frank Sinatra tribute nights.

6 The Broadway
734 East Broadway, South Boston

On weekends this watering hole is packed both inside and outside in the garden. Modern pub food hits a fairly high mark.

7 L Street Tavern
658A East 8th St, South Boston

One of Southie's most old-fashioned pubs, L Street serves Harpoon and Guinness on tap. The Oscar-winning movie *Good Will Hunting* was filmed here.

8 Brendan Behan Pub
378 Centre St, Jamaica Plain

This Irish pub, named after the Irish playwright Brendan Behan, is one of the treasured gems in the city. Visit for a pint of beer and live music, and stay for the charming ambience.

9 Local 149
149 P St, South Boston

This South Boston neighborhood joint features local beers on tap, creative cocktails, and some of the best New American food outside of a fancy restaurant.

10 The Haven
2 Perkins St, Jamaica Plain

One of the city's most active purveyors of Scottish craft beers, ales, and ciders, The Haven also boasts an extensive single malt whisky collection. Do not miss the fine lamb haggis.

Bar at The Haven

Restaurants

① Coppersmith
40 W 3rd St, South Boston ▪ 617 658 3452 ▪ $$

Set in a vast converted warehouse, Coppersmith houses an American bistro restaurant as well as a casual café serving global fare. Try the excellent BBQ popcorn.

Bright decor at Tres Gatos

② Tres Gatos
470 Centre St, Jamaica Plain ▪ 617 477 4851 ▪ $

This part tapas bar, part book and music store features authentic Spanish bar dishes along with some inventive variants.

③ Yellow Door Taqueria
2297 Dorchester Ave ▪ 857 267 4201 ▪ Closed L ▪ $

Specializing in craft cocktails, rare tequila, and local beer, this snazzy Mexican bar in Lower Mills serves innovative tacos, healthy salads, and great ceviches.

④ Ashmont Grill
MAP D4 ▪ 555 Talbot Ave, Dorchester ▪ 617 825 4300 ▪ Closed B, L Mon–Fri ▪ $$

Veteran chef Chris Douglass uses local produce to conjure up contemporary bistro delights at this rustic restaurant.

⑤ El Miami Restaurant
381 Centre St, Jamaica Plain ▪ 617 522 4644 ▪ $

This place is the self-proclaimed "King of the Cuban sandwiches." Check out the photos of the Latin American pro baseball players who often eat here when in town.

⑥ Tavolo Dot Ave
1918 Dorchester Ave, Dorchester ▪ 617 822 1918 ▪ Closed L ▪ $$

An Ashmont neighborhood staple, Tavolo serves market-fresh and rustic Italian dishes.

⑦ Ten Tables
597 Centre St, Jamaica Plain ▪ 617 524 8810 ▪ Closed L ▪ $$$

A small venue with just ten tables, this restaurant has an equally compact but rewarding menu, such as scallops on minted pea tendrils.

⑧ Vee Vee
763 Centre St, Jamaica Plain ▪ 617 522 0145 ▪ Closed L & Mon ▪ $$$

Delectable American bistro fare makes this restaurant a favorite with local foodies, especially since many dishes have vegetarian versions. The Sunday brunch is very popular.

⑨ Brassica Kitchen + Cafe
3710 Washington St, Jamaica Plain ▪ 617 477 4519 ▪ $

Rumor has it that Brassica serves Boston's best fried chicken. Order and decide for yourself. Expect a pastry-centric menu if you are visiting at breakfast or brunch time

⑩ Blue Nile
389 Centre St, Jamaica Plain ▪ 617 522 6453 ▪ Closed Mon ▪ $

Vegetables take center stage in the Ethiopian home-style dishes served here, but there are also plenty of meat and fish options. *Teff injera*, the sourdough pancakes that double as utensils, are made on the premises.

See map on p130 ⟵

Streetsmart

Boston street signs

Getting Around

Arriving by Air

Logan International Airport (BOS), served by almost 50 international and domestic airlines, is located 2 miles (3 km) northeast of Downtown Boston. Transportation to central Boston is accessed from the baggage claim area. Free buses link terminals to the Blue Line subway and South Station (via the free MBTA Silver Line bus). Taxis wait at all terminals but airport fees can make rides expensive ($25–$35). Logan Airport is also served by private taxi companies, such as **Star Shuttle**, as well as ride sharing companies. Shuttle services are available via **Massport** to locations in Downtown Boston and to eastern Massachusetts.

For the scenic water route, take the Route 66 airport shuttle to Logan Dock. **Boston Water Taxi** serves Logan and the waterfront. **Rowes Wharf Water Transport** provides direct service to and from Rowes Wharf.

Several international and some domestic char-ters use **Manchester Airport** (MHT) in New Hampshire, 50 miles (79 km) from Boston, and **TF Green Airport** (PVD), near Providence, Rhode Island, 59 miles (95 km) from Boston. Buses to Boston run from both.

Arriving by Rail

The **Amtrak** intercity rail transportation arrives into Boston at South Station (Atlantic and Summer streets) from various other cities in the US. Rail services from New York take three to five hours and are very frequent.

Amtrak also connects Boston with the rest of New England. The Northeast Regional route, which departs from South Station, connects the city to Long Island Sound, Connecticut, and Providence. Amtrak's daily Downeaster service leaves Boston's North Station, with stops in New Hampshire, and ends in Brunswick, Maine.

Arriving by Bus

The city's primary bus station, **South Station Transportation Center**, is used by a dozen com-panies providing intercity services, and is part of Amtrak and the MBTA subway system. **Greyhound** offers low-cost routes between Boston and many US cities. Other lines include **Megabus**, **BoltBus**, and Peter Pan.

Traveling by Water

Cruise ships dock at Black Falcon Terminal, South Boston, which is a $25 taxi ride away from Downtown. On Port of Call days, the local trolley tour companies *(see p143)* offer services to popular city destinations.

Boston Harbor Cruises runs ferries to Salem and Provincetown from Long Wharf. The **Bay State Cruise Company** connects the World Trade Center with Provincetown, and the inexpensive

MBTA Harbor Express links Long Wharf to Charlestown Navy Yard.

Public Transportation

The Massachusetts Bay Transportation Authority (**MBTA**) operates the subway (known more commonly as the "T") and bus lines in the Metropolitan Boston area as well as commuter rail options stretching north to Newburyport, west to Worcester, and south to Providence, Rhode Island. Safety and hygiene measures, timetables, ticket information, transportation maps, and more can be obtained from the MBTA website.

Tickets

Fares and ticket options for the MBTA network vary depending on the form of transportation. There are four ways to purchase a ticket: with cash, the electronic mTicket app, a plastic CharlieCard, or a paper CharlieTicket.

Use cash to buy bus, subway, trolley, ferry, and commuter rail tickets via the onboard fare boxes or street-level stops.

Android and iPhone users can download the mTicket app, and use it to purchase tickets and passes for travel on ferries and commuter rail lines.

Intended largely for residents, CharlieCards are only valid for travel on the city's buses, subway, and Silver Line.

CharlieTickets can be purchased at any MBTA vending machine and loaded with a single trip ($2.40 subway/$1.70 bus), a 24-hour pass ($12.75) or 7-day pass ($22.50). CharlieTickets that are loaded with a single trip are only valid on buses, the subway, and the Silver Line, while those loaded with a pass can be used throughout Boston's public transportation system. This is the best option for visitors planning on traveling around the city.

Bus

The MBTA bus system covers most of the city. Two useful sightseeing routes are Haymarket–Charlestown (from near Quincy Market to Bunker Hill) and Harvard–Nubian (from Harvard Square via Massachusetts Avenue to Back Bay and South End to Nubian Square). The Silver Line, which provides quick trips to airport or cruise ship terminals, is also convenient. Maps are available on the MBTA website or at the office at Downtown Crossing.

Subway

Boston's combined subway and trolley network, known as the "T", is run by the MBTA. It operates 5am–12:45am daily (from 6am on Sundays). Weekday service is every 3–15 minutes; note that it is less frequent at weekends. There are five lines: Red, from south of the city to Cambridge; Green, from the Museum of Science westward into the suburbs; Blue, from near Government Center to Logan International Airport and on to Revere; Orange, linking the northern suburbs to southwest Boston; and Silver, a surface bus that runs from Roxbury to Logan International Airport via South Station.

Maps of Boston's subway system are available at Downtown Crossing MBTA station, or online.

Taxis

Due to the popularity of Lyft and Uber ride-hailing services, taxicabs are becoming increasingly scarce, though cabs can still be hired on the street in the Downtown area or at taxi stands. You can also call **Metro Cab**, **Boston Cab Association**, **ITOA**, or **Cambridge Cabs** to arrange a pick up.

Note that cab companies that operate in the Boston Metropolitan area are limited to picking up in the cities where they are chartered. A Boston cab cannot pick up in Cambridge or vice versa.

DIRECTORY

ARRIVING BY AIR

Boston Water Taxi
w bostonharbor cruises.com

Logan International Airport
w massport.com

Manchester Airport
w flymanchester.com

Massport
w massport.com

Rowes Wharf Water Transport
w roweswharfwater transport.com

Star Shuttle
w starshuttleboston.com

TF Green Airport
w pvdairport.com

ARRIVING BY RAIL

Amtrak
w amtrak.com

ARRIVING BY BUS

BoltBus
w boltbus.com

Greyhound
w greyhound.com

Megabus
w megabus.com

Peter Pan
w peterpanbus.com

South Station Transportation Center
w south-station.net

TRAVELING BY WATER

Bay State Cruise Company
w baystatecruise company.com

Boston Harbor Cruises
w bostonharborcruises. com

MBTA Harbor Express
w mbta.com

PUBLIC TRANSPORTATION

MBTA
w mbta.com

TAXIS

Boston Cab Association
w bostoncab.us

Cambridge Cabs
w cambridgecabs.info

ITOA
w itoataxi.com

Metro Cab
w boston-cab.com

Driving to Boston

The I-95 superhighway (also known as Route 128) is the main entry to New England from New York and points south. This major highway runs close to the coast through Connecticut and Providence, and Rhode Island to the outskirts of Boston, where it bypasses the city center. Here, it connects with roads into the city.

The I-90, also known as the Massachusetts Turnpike, is the main route into the city from the west.

From the north, the I-89 starts in northwestern Vermont, then cuts diagonally from Burlington to Concord, New Hampshire, where it links up with I-93 into Boston. I-93 crosses the city north to south as an underground expressway, known as the Thomas P. "Tip" O'Neill Jr. Tunnel. Watch signs carefully for exits. The Zakim bridge, connecting underground and surface highways, provides a northern gateway to Boston.

Driving in Boston

The least efficient way to get around Downtown is driving, which can be stressful. The narrow streets are laid out in a confusing manner with little signage. There are few gas stations, limited parking with time-of-day restrictions, and many one-way streets and traffic circles.

If you do decide to travel by car in Boston, and are unfamiliar with the city, an up-to-date GPS and advance planning are essential for ensuring a stress-free experience.

Parking lots are very expensive, costing about $35 per day or about $12 for one hour in the Boston Common Garage in the city center. Other parking lots in the area charge more. It is cheaper to park on-street. Note, however, that on-street parking meters have a two-hour limit, residents-only rules are strictly enforced, and fines are high.

It is far easier to drive outside the city. Divided highways connect Boston to New England's other major cities and provide endless opportunities for diversions along scenic open roads, passing through pretty rural and seaside settlements. Rural New England rewards road trippers, especially during fall foliage season, when the region's roads are fringed by golden, red, and orange leaves. Summer is also a great time to hit the road, although heavy traffic can slow progress on popular roads during peak season. Winter and early spring driving have their challenges. Snow and ice call for special driving skills, and frost heaves create sidewalk cracks and potholes.

Car Rental

To rent a car in Boston you must be between 21 and 75 years old, and have a valid credit card and license. Some rental companies charge an extra fee to drivers under the age of 25.

Major international car rental agencies, including **Enterprise**, **Hertz**, and **Avis** have outlets at Logan Airport, as well as elsewhere in the city.

Collision damage waiver and liability insurances are often not included but are highly recommended.

Rules of the Road

Third party insurance is required and you should always carry your policy documents and driving license in the vehicle.

Drive on the right. Pass only on the outside or left-hand lane, and when approaching a traffic circle, give priority to traffic already on the circle. All vehicles must give way to emergency services vehicles.

Seat belts must be worn at all times by the driver and passengers of the vehicle. Young children should be restrained in child seats buckled into the back seat.

In Boston, and the rest of Massachusetts, it is against the law to use a hand-held electronic device while driving, except in an emergency. If you are traveling around New England, note that laws vary on using a cell phone while driving; err on the side of caution and pull over to call or text.

The legal blood alcohol limit for drivers is 0.08 per cent. Avoid drinking alcohol completely if you plan to drive.

Cycling

Compared to other US cities, Boston has an excellent cycling infrastructure. Bike sharing scheme **Bluebikes** operates at stations throughout Boston and Cambridge. Central Boston and Cambridge have many bike lanes along major city streets, including Dutch-style protected lanes. Otherwise, it is legal to pedal on city streets, though cycling on highways is illegal. Riding on sidewalks is permitted only when moving at a walking pace, and you should always give way to pedestrians.

Boston also offers a surprising number of opportunities for off-road cycling. A designated bike path runs through the verdant **Southwest Corridor Park** and a circular, cycling-friendly loop takes in the **Emerald Necklace** chain of parks. Want to take in the waterfront? There are paths around the Charles River basin between the Charles River Dam and Watertown. If you're traveling with kids, a good option is the **Minuteman Bikeway**, a paved bike path on a former rail line which links Cambridge, Arlington, Lexington, Concord, and Bedford. As no vehicles are allowed to travel along the bikeway, it is safe for even the most unsteady of cyclists.

Beyond the city, New England offers many options for cyclists of all ages and abilities. Trails in state parks and national parks forests are perfect off-road riding territory, and most ski resorts permit mountain biking (for a fee) in the summer. The **Massachusetts Department of Conservation and Recreation** has information on trails

within the state, while **Bike New England** has compiled guides to cycling across the region.

Several companies, including **VBT**, operate guided and self-guided cycling tours around New England.

Helmets and high-visibility clothing are not obligatory but wearing them is strongly advised, especially when cycling on rural roads.

Walking and Hiking

Downtown Boston is compact and easy to get around on foot. Stay on sidewalks and cross only at marked intersections. Several companies run walking tours and there are even routes for particular interests like movies or food (see p145).

For a very urbanized city, Boston also has some excellent hiking and walking trails. Chief among them is the 43-mile (69-km) waterfront path known as the **Boston Harborwalk**. It stretches from the Neponset River in the south around the harbor to Belle Isle Marsh, which sits to the east of Logan Airport. Another excellent walking destination is the Arnold Arboretum (see p131). This preserve is criss-crossed with walking trails and is especially striking during the fall foliage season, when the trees put on one of nature's greatest shows.

For hiking trails outside the city proper, check out **Trustees of Reservations**, which protects landscapes and landmarks across

Massachusetts. See the website for details on individual reservations and routes.

If going off the beaten path, take good hiking boots, waterproof outerwear, warm inner clothing, a map, and a compass. Make sure your phone is fully charged but don't count on having cell service in remote areas, so tell friends or family what route you're planning on taking.

DIRECTORY

CAR RENTAL

Avis
w avis.com

Enterprise
w enterprise.com

Hertz
w hertz.com

CYCLING

Bike New England
w bikenewengland.com

Bluebikes
w bluebikes.com

Emerald Necklace
w emeraldnecklace.org

Massachusetts Department of Conservation and Recreation
w mass.gov/find-dcr-rail-trails-and-other-shared-use-paths

Minuteman Bikeway
w minutemanbikeway.org

Southwest Corridor Park
w swcpc.org/bicycling.asp

VBT
w vbt.com

WALKING AND HIKING

Boston Harborwalk
w bostonharbornow.org

Trustees of Reservations
w thetrustees.org

Practical Information

Passports and Visas

For entry requirements, including visas, consult your nearest US embassy or check with the **US Department of State**. All travelers to the US should have a machine-readable biometric passport that is valid for six months longer than their intended period of stay. Visitors from Canada, Mexico, and Bermuda require no other documentation to enter the US. Citizens of the UK, Australia, New Zealand, and the EU do not need a visa, but must apply to enter in advance via the **Electronic System for Travel Authorization (ESTA)**. Applications must be made at least 72 hours before travel, and applicants must have a return airline ticket. All other visitors require a tourist visa to enter. Be sure to allow plenty of time for the US border agency's thorough identity checks.

Government Advice

Now more than ever, it is important to consult both your and the US government's advice before traveling. The US Department of State, the **UK Foreign and Commonwealth Office**, and the **Australian Department of Foreign Affairs and Trade** offer the latest information on security, health, and local regulations.

Customs Information

You can find information on the laws relating to goods and currency taken in or out of the US on the **Customs and Border Protection Agency** website. All travelers need to complete a Customs and Border Protection Agency form when crossing the US border.

Insurance

We recommend that you take out a comprehensive insurance policy covering theft, loss of belongings, medical care, cancellations, and delays, and read the small print carefully. All medical treatment is private and US health insurers do not have reciprocal arrangements with other countries. Car rental agencies offer vehicle and liability insurance, but always check your policy.

Health

The US does not have a government health program, so emergency medical and dental care, though excellent, can be very expensive. Medical travel insurance is highly recommended in order to cover some of the costs related to an accident or sudden illness. The price of basic care at a hospital emergency room can rise incredibly quickly. Should you be in a serious accident, an ambulance will pick you up and charge later.

Hospitals such as the **Massachusetts General Hospital**, **Boston Medical Center**, **Tufts Medical Center**, **Partners Urgent Care**, and **Beth Israel Deaconess Medical Center** offer emergency and urgent walk-in care. Minor injury clinics such as those run by **CVS** are available through the city and central Boston has a CVS 24-hour Pharmacy.

For information regarding COVID-19 vaccination requirements, consult government advice.

Unless otherwise stated, tap water is drinkable.

Smoking, Alcohol, and Drugs

Smoking and "vaping" are banned in all public spaces such as bus and train stations, airports, and in enclosed areas of bars, cafes, restaurants, and hotels. However, many bars and restaurants have outdoor areas where smoking is permitted.

Alcohol may not be sold to or bought for anyone under the age of 21. The drink-drive limit is strictly enforced (see p140). Recreational cannabis use is legal in Massachusetts.

ID

Passports are required as ID at airports. (American citizens may use a state driver's license to board domestic flights.) Anyone who looks under 25 may be asked for photo ID to prove their age when buying alcohol or tobacco.

Personal Security

Boston is a relatively safe city to visit, but petty crime does take place. Pickpockets work known tourist areas and busy streets. Use your common sense, keep valuables in a safe place, and be alert to your surroundings.

If you have anything stolen, report the crime as soon as possible to the **Boston Police Department**. Get a copy a of the crime report to claim on your insurance. Within the MBTA's service area, you can also ask the **MBTA Transit Police** for help. Contact your embassy or consulate immediately if your passport is stolen or in the event of a serious crime or accident.

For **ambulance, medical, police, and fire brigade** services, call 911 and give your location and details about the problem.

As a rule, Bostonians are very accepting of all people, regardless of their race, gender, or sexuality. The country's abolitionist and women's suffrage movements both started here, and Massachusetts was the first state in the United States to legalize same-sex marriage (in 2004). Today, Boston has the largest LGBTQ+ population in the state, but even small towns are accepting. If you do feel unsafe, the **Safe Space Alliance** pinpoints your nearest place of refuge.

Travelers with Specific Requirements

The **Society for Accessible Travel and Hospitality** and **Mobility International** offer information for people with disabilities.

All facilities renovated or newly built since 1987 are legally required to provide wheelchair-accessible entrances and restrooms. Government buildings, museums, and theaters are accessible, but call ahead to verify that tours can meet your needs. It is best to call historic buildings, hotels, and restaurants in advance to ask about amenities. The website of the **Greater Boston Convention & Visitors Bureau** has access information and contact numbers for a range of places and tours.

All establishments allow service animals, and most busy road intersections have audio signals for safe crossing times.

Most MBTA *(see p139)* commuter rail lines, buses, subways, and ferries accommodate wheelchairs; check website for details. The Boston Cab Association *(see p139)* will send an accessible vehicle on request. Logan International Airport *(see p139)* has accessible ramps, elevators, and restrooms, plus a list of accessible transportation to and from the airport on its website.

DIRECTORY

PASSPORTS AND VISAS

Electronic System for Travel Authorization (ESTA)
w esta.cbp.dhs.gov/esta

US Department of State
w travel.state.gov

GOVERNMENT ADVICE

Australian Department of Foreign Affairs and Trade
w smartraveller.gov.au

UK Foreign and Commonwealth Office
w gov.uk/foreign-travel-advice

CUSTOMS INFORMATION

Customs and Border Protection Agency
w cbp.gov/travel

HEALTH

Beth Israel Deaconess Medical Center
w bidmc.org

Boston Medical Center
w bmc.org

CVS
w cvs.com

Massachusetts General Hospital
w massgeneral.org

Partners Urgent Care
w partnersurgentcare.org

Tufts Medical Center
w tuftsmedicalcenter.org

PERSONAL SECURITY

Ambulance, Medical, Police, and Fire Brigade
c 911

Boston Police Department
c 617 343 4500

MBTA Transit Police
c 617 222 1212

Safe Space Alliance
w safespacealliance.com

TRAVELERS WITH SPECIFIC REQUIREMENTS

Greater Boston Convention & Visitors Bureau
w bostonusa.com/plan/transportation/getting-around/accessibility

Mobility International
w miusa.org

Society for Accessible Travel and Hospitality
w sath.org

Time Zone

Boston is on Eastern Standard Time (EST). Daylight Saving Time starts at 2am on the second Sunday in March and ends on the first Sunday in November.

Money

The US currency is the dollar ($). Most establishments accept major credit, debit, and prepaid currency cards. Contactless payments are becoming widely accepted, however, it is always worth carrying some cash for smaller items and tips. Cash machines can be found at banks, airline terminals, train and bus stations, and on main streets.

Waiters will expect to be tipped 15 to 20 per cent of the total bill, hotel porters and housekeeping should be given $1 per bag or day, and you should round up taxi fares to the nearest dollar.

Electrical Appliances

The standard US electric current is 110 volts and 60 Hz current. An adapter will be required for all European appliances.

Cell Phones and Wi-Fi

If you plan to use a cell phone, check with your provider about service in the US before traveling. Canadian residents can usually upgrade their domestic cell phone plan to extend to the US. Visitors from outside North America can buy a pay-as-you-go SIM card at most phone stores, which can be used in compatible phones. **Cellular Abroad**, **Cellhire**, and others rent phones, and some networks also sell basic flip phones for as little as $25 (no paperwork or ID required). Pre-paid phone cards usually offer the best rates for long-distance calls, and are sold in most drugstores.

Free Wi-Fi hotspots are widely available. Almost all hotels, motels, and inns also offer free Wi-Fi, as do many cafes, bars, and restaurants.

Postal Services

Flat rate envelopes and boxes for all destinations are available at **US Postal Service** post offices.

Weather

Summers can be humid and hot (over 81° F/27° C), while winters can be very cold (as low as 21° F/-6° C) with snow, ice, and wind. Spring and fall weather is generally pleasant, with warm days and cool mornings and evenings.

Opening Hours

Office hours are 9am to 5pm. Stores open at 10am or 11am and close at 6pm or 7pm Monday to Saturday, while on Sunday hours are usually noon to 6pm. Most banks are open 9am to 4pm or 5pm Monday to Friday, and some also open on Saturday morning. Museums are usually open 10am (noon on Sun) to 5pm, but check before making your plans.

MBTA trains begin at about 5am Monday to Saturday, 6am on Sunday, and end between midnight and 1am every night. Each line and each station varies so check ahead.

COVID-19 Increased rates of infection may result in temporary opening hours and/or closures. Always check ahead before visiting museums, attractions, and hospitality venues.

Visitor Information

The **Greater Boston Convention & Visitors Bureau** has information on hotels, shops, dining, sights, and transportation on its website, and at the Boston Common Visitor Center and information booth at Copley Place. The **Boston National Historical Park** visitor center at Faneuil Hall also has plenty of information.

The **Cambridge Office of Tourism** has an inter-active website and an information booth in Harvard Square. The **City of Boston** website and the **Massachusetts Office of Travel & Tourism** are also useful resources.

Many of Boston's museums, galleries, and attractions offer discounts to students and senior citizens. Students from abroad should carry an International Student Identity Card (**ISIC**) to claim discounts on hostel accommodation, museums, and theaters. Over-50s should look into buying an **AARP** membership (open to non-Americans), which can provide discounts at hotels and on car rentals.

Trips and Tours

Several trolley tours start near the Boston Common Visitor Center, including **Old Town Trolley Tours** and **City View Trolley Tours**, which offer narrated sightseeing on old-fashioned trolley buses. Boston Harbor Cruises (see p139) offers harbor and whale-watching tours. Sightseeing and sunset tours of the Charles River are offered by the **Charles Riverboat Company** and **Boston Duck Tours**, which uses open-topped amphibious vehicles that both trundle through the streets and plunge into the Charles River.

Enthusiastic volunteers from **Boston By Foot** share their love of the city on a range of guided walks. **Bites of Boston** offers tastings, tips, and insights on the city's food markets, restaurants, and cuisines.

Free Tours by Foot explores the Freedom Trail, the Battle of Bunker Hill, Kennedy family sights, and Boston's Irish history.

Urban Adventours runs narrated bicycle tours that include the city's highlights, a ride along the Charles River at sunset, or a fall foliage tour through the Emerald Necklace.

Movie buffs will enjoy a walk to iconic Boston film and television locations with **On Location Tours**.

Language

English is the principal language spoken in Boston, although you might hear Italian, Mandarin, and Cantonese in some parts of the city.

Taxes and Refunds

The Massachusetts sales tax is 6.25 per cent of the price or rental charge, excluding prescription medicines, groceries, gasoline, and clothing (under the value of $175). As taxes are levied by the state, international visitors cannot claim refunds.

Accommodations

Boston offers a huge variety of accommodations. You can even stay overnight on a tall ship moored in Boston Harbor with **Liberty Fleet**. The Greater Boston Convention & Visitors Bureau has a comprehensive list of hotels. For bed-and-breakfast properties, contact the **Bed and Breakfast Agency of Boston**.

To find the best price, check online and then call the hotel to ask for its best rate. Hotel tax in the Boston area is 14.15 per cent, and room rates are usually quoted without tax.

DIRECTORY

CELL PHONES AND WI-FI

Cellhire
🅦 cellhire.com

Cellular Abroad
🅦 cellularabroad.com

POSTAL SERVICES

US Postal Service
🅦 usps.com

VISITOR INFORMATION

AARP
🅦 aarp.org

Boston National Historical Park
🅦 nps.gov/bost

Cambridge Office of Tourism
🅦 cambridgeusa.org

City of Boston
🅦 cityofboston.gov

Greater Boston Convention & Visitors Bureau
🅦 bostonusa.com

ISIC
🅦 isic.org

Massachusetts Office of Travel & Tourism
🅦 massvacation.com

TRIPS AND TOURS

Bites of Boston
🅦 bitesofbostonfoodtours.com

Boston By Foot
🅦 bostonbyfoot.org

Boston Duck Tours
🅦 bostonducktours.com

Charles Riverboat Company
🅦 charlesriverboat.com

City View Trolley Tours
🅦 cityviewtrolleys.com

Free Tours by Foot
🅦 freetoursbyfoot.com

Old Town Trolley Tours
🅦 trolleytours.com/boston

On Location Tours
🅦 onlocationtours.com/boston-movie-tv-tours

Urban Adventours
🅦 urbanadventours.com

ACCOMMODATIONS

Bed and Breakfast Agency of Boston
🅦 boston-bnbagency.com

Liberty Fleet
🅦 libertyfleet.com

Places to Stay

> **PRICE CATEGORIES**
> For a standard, double room per night (with breakfast if included), taxes and extra charges.
>
> $ under $250 $$ $250 to $450 $$$ over $450

Luxury Hotels

Eliot Hotel
MAP J5 ■ 370 Commonwealth Ave, 02215 ■ 617 267 1607 ■ www.eliothotel.com ■ $$
Back Bay grace and charm characterize this late 19th-century landmark hotel. Visiting musicians and baseball teams alike enjoy the spacious suites. Uni *(see p93)*, the ground-floor restaurant, is one of Boston's most acclaimed and provides room service for the Eliot's guests.

Liberty Hotel
MAP F3 ■ 215 Charles St, 02114 ■ 617 224 4000 ■ www.libertyhotel.com ■ $$
Located at the foot of Beacon Hill, this swanky hotel incorporates the historic granite architecture of the Charles Street Jail in modern design. Basketball and hockey teams stay here, as TD Garden is nearby.

Boston Harbor Hotel
MAP R3 ■ 70 Rowes Wharf, 02110 ■ 617 439 7000 ■ www.bhh.com ■ $$$
To enjoy one of the most beautiful locations in the city to the full, request a room with a harbor view and a private balcony. There's no need to go anywhere else as you will find restaurants, a fitness center, and spa all on site.

Four Seasons
MAP E5 ■ 1 Dalton St, 02115 ■ 617 377 4888 ■ www.fourseasons.com ■ $$$
Towering over the city, Four Seasons offers spacious and airy rooms fitted with modern amenities. Zuma, a Japanese restaurant housed here, offers great *Izakaya*.

Langham, Boston
MAP Q3 ■ 250 Franklin St, 02110 ■ 617 451 1900 ■ www.langhamhotels.com ■ $$$
Reopened in 2020 after an extensive renovation, the sophisticated Langham occupies an Art Nouveau building. Spacious rooms and a seamless service characterize this hotel.

Mandarin Oriental
MAP K6 ■ 776 Boylston St, 02199 ■ 617 535 8888 ■ www.mandarinoriental.com ■ $$$
Situated in the heart of Back Bay, this hotel has some of the largest and most luxurious rooms in the city, furnished with huge bathtubs, designer linens, and state-of-the-art electronics. Many guests stay on site just to enjoy the full-service spa.

The Newbury
MAP M4 ■ 15 Arlington St, 02116 ■ 617 536 5700 ■ www.thenewburyboston.com ■ $$$
Built in 1927, The Newbury benefits from being in a great location – at the juncture of Back Bay and Beacon Hill. This hotel epitomizes opulence as well as "old Boston" style, and has freshly renovated rooms that prioritize comfort. The lobby bar is legendary.

Nine Zero
MAP G3–G4 ■ 90 Tremont St, 02108 ■ 617 722 5800 ■ www.ninezerohotel.com ■ $$$
Marrying sleek steel, chrome, and glass with warm wood and designer furniture, Nine Zero achieves a contemporary look with a soft edge. Its location on the Downtown Crossing corner of Boston Common is convenient.

Ritz-Carlton, Boston Common
MAP N4 ■ 10 Avery St, 02111 ■ 617 574 7100 ■ www.ritzcarlton.com ■ $$$
This classy hotel is on the upper levels of the tallest building overlooking the Common. The rooms offer a wealth of high-tech and luxury amenities. The hotel complex also has a full-service spa.

The Whitney Hotel
MAP F3 ■ 170 Charles St, 02114 ■ 888 673 3650 ■ www.whitneyhotelboston.com ■ $$$
Set at the river end of Beacon Hill's Charles Street, the suave Whitney Hotel – a pet-friendly, boutique establishment – embodies the charm of the neighborhood's famous townhouses. Some suites have sweeping river views.

XV Beacon
MAP P3 ▪ 15 Beacon St, 02108 ▪ 617 670 1500 ▪ www.xvbeacon.com ▪ $$$

Set in a handsome Beaux Arts building, XV Beacon is a luxury boutique hotel that provides impeccable service and a range of modern comforts. This hotel has 63 spacious rooms that are equipped with high-tech amenities.

Deluxe Hotels

Battery Wharf Hotel
MAP H2 ▪ 3 Battery Wharf, 02109 ▪ 617 994 9000 ▪ www.battery wharfhotelboston.com ▪ $$

Right on the Boston Harborwalk, this suave hotel has spacious rooms and suites, many with stunning harbor views. It is located very close to TD Garden arena. The Quincy Market is also at a walking distance.

The Colonnade
MAP K6 ▪ 120 Huntington Ave, 02116 ▪ 617 424 7000 ▪ www.colonnade hotel.com ▪ $$

Often used by upscale tour groups, the Colonnade has some of the largest and most comfortable rooms in Back Bay, as well as an outdoor rooftop pool.

Element Boston
MAP D5 ▪ 1 391–5 D. St, 02210 ▪ 617 530 1700 ▪ www.marriott.com ▪ $$

Located close to Boston's cruise terminal and the Convention and Exhibition Center, this minimalist hotel promises absolute comfort. There are also amenities such as a fitness center and an indoor pool. For a visit that focuses on the Seaport District, Element is the perfect choice.

The Godfrey Hotel
MAP P4 ▪ 2505 Washington St, 02111 ▪ 617 804 2000 ▪ www. godfreyhotelboston.com ▪ $$

The Godfrey is set in a historical Downtown Crossing building and houses stylish and serene rooms. It is perfectly located for sightseeing around the city.

Hotel Marlowe
MAP F2 ▪ 25 Edwin H. Land Blvd, Cambridge, 02141 ▪ 617 868 8000 ▪ www.hotelmarlowe. com ▪ $$

Set behind the Museum of Science, this sleek hotel creates a self-contained world of comfort with in-room spa services, evening wine receptions, and a fitness center.

Klimpton Onyx Hotel
MAP P4 ▪ 155 Portland St, 02114 ▪ 617 557 9955 ▪ www.onyxhotel. com ▪ $$

Situated between the TD Garden and Faneuil Hall, this casually elegant hotel features artful accents and has a family-friendly ambience. Guests can borrow hotel bikes and Wi-Fi is free for members of the IHG loyalty program.

Revere Hotel
MAP N5 ▪ 200 Stuart St, 02116 ▪ 617 428 1800 ▪ www.reverehotel.com ▪ $$

This sleek, hip hotel is located near the Boston Common. Every room has a private balcony. The bar serves lunch in summer by the pool-side.

Royal Sonesta
MAP F2 ▪ 40 Edwin H. Land Blvd, Cambridge, 02142 ▪ 617 806 4200 ▪ www.sonesta.com ▪ $$

An excellent restaurant, outstanding art collection, and striking riverside location make Royal Sonesta a top choice for aesthetes. Family packages available in summer are a great bargain.

Seaport Hotel
1 Seaport Lane, 02210 ▪ 617 385 4000 ▪ www. seaportboston.com ▪ $$

Connected by a walkway to the World Trade Center, the Seaport was one of the first to pioneer the South Boston Waterfront. Rooms are comfortable, and the pool is a bonus. The hotel is located near a MBTA Silver Line stop.

The Verb Hotel
MAP D5 ▪ 1271 Boylston St, 02215 ▪ 617 566 4500 ▪ www.theverbhotel.com ▪ $$

In the shadow of the iconic Fenway Park, the retro-themed Verb hotel is in demand whenever there's a big event around the corner. The stylish atmosphere and location attract younger crowds looking to celebrate.

The Bostonian Boston
MAP Q2 ▪ Faneuil Hall Marketplace, 02109 ▪ 617 523 3600 ▪ www. millenniumhotels.com ▪ $$$

Rooms run the gamut from tiny to palatial in this swanky oasis close to bustling Faneuil Hall and Quincy Market (see p101), but all feature lovely city views. There is also an on-site fitness center.

The Charles Hotel
MAP B2 ▪ 1 Bennett St, Cambridge, 02138 ▪ 617 864 1200 ▪ www.charles hotel.com ▪ $$$

Extra touches, such as handmade quilts hanging on the walls, personalize the comfortable rooms at this modern hotel on the edge of Harvard Square. There's an indoor pool, an outstanding jazz club – the Reggatabar (see p128) – and the restaurant Henrietta's Table serves regional foods.

Marriott Long Wharf
MAP R2 ▪ 296 State St, 02109 ▪ 617 227 0800 ▪ www.marriottlong wharf.com ▪ $$$

The waterfront location means most of the bright, spacious rooms have superb harbor or city views. Waterline, the casual bar-restaurant, is perfect for a cocktail.

Hip/Historic Stays

The Boxer Boston
MAP P2 ▪ 107 Merrimac St, 02114 ▪ 617 624 0202 ▪ www.theboxerboston. com ▪ $$

This stylish boutique hotel offers rooms and suites that show off a sleek "industrial chic" design and are equipped with all the latest amenities. The Boxer is centrally located between North End and Beacon Hill – ideal for exploring the city on foot.

The Envoy Hotel
MAP R4 ▪ 70 Sleeper St, 02118 ▪ 617 338 3030 ▪ www.theenvoyhotel. com ▪ $$$

Set in the Seaport District, near the Institute of Contemporary Art, the Envoy unabashedly courts youthful techies and legal executives with its millennial-friendly design. The stunning rooftop bar is a popular date spot.

Hotel InterContinental
MAP H4 ▪ 510 Atlantic Ave, 02110 ▪ 617 217 5030 ▪ www.interconti nentalboston.com ▪ $$

This chic waterfront hotel at the edge of Fort Point Channel combines sophisticated architecture with luxurious decor of rich furnishings and textiles. Sumptuous bathrooms include a soaking tub as well as a walk-in shower.

Hotel Veritas
MAP C2 ▪ 1 Remington St, Cambridge, 02138 ▪ 617 520 5000 ▪ www. thehotelveritas.com ▪ $$

A luxury four-story boutique hotel located near Harvard, Veritas is ideally sited for families visiting students. Combining opulence with convenience – rooms are intimate and contemporary, and bathrooms have marble finishes. A cozy lounge in the lobby serves cocktails.

Loews Boston Hotel
MAP F5 ▪ 350 Stuart St, 02116 ▪ 617 266 7200 ▪ www.loewshotels.com/ boston-hotel ▪ $$

This posh boutique hotel in the handsome limestone former Boston police headquarters offers deluxe comfort and services in a convenient corner of South End.

Moxy Boston Downtown
MAP P4 ▪ 240 Tremont St, 02116 ▪ 617 793 4200 ▪ www.marriott. com ▪ $$

Colorful, young, and hip, the Moxy Boston sits on a Theater District corner of Chinatown. It is frankly marketed as a party hotel with vivid public spaces and compact, minimalist rooms, with walk-in showers and free high-speed Wi-Fi.

W Hotel
MAP G5 ▪ 100 Stuart St, 02116 ▪ 617 261 8700 ▪ www.marriott.com ▪ $$

Seemingly designed as much for the architectural press as for the traveler, W appeals to visitors who enjoy the convenient location in the Theater District at the edge of Back Bay. A Bliss Spa located in the hotel is the ideal place to relax.

Boston Park Plaza
MAP M5 ▪ 50 Park Plaza, 02116 ▪ 617 426 2000 ▪ www.bostonparkplaza. com ▪ $$$

The Park Plaza, built in 1927, is Boston's largest historic hotel. Sensitive restoration has carefully reinstated some of its old glamour. Popular with convention-goers, tour packagers, and business travelers, it is convenient for Back Bay and the Theater District.

Fairmont Copley Plaza
MAP L5 ▪ 138 St James Ave, 02116 ▪ 617 267 5300 ▪ www.fairmont. com ▪ $$$

The sister hotel of New York's Plaza, the Copley

Plaza has been a Copley Square landmark since 1912. The public areas of the Fairmont are opulent. Its rooms may be small, however, they are very comfortable, and its suites are truly grand.

Hotel Commonwealth
MAP D5 ▪ 500 Commonwealth Ave, 02215 ▪ 617 933 5000 ▪ www.hotelcommon wealth.com ▪ $$$
Right by Kenmore Square, this suave 245-room hotel has all the high-tech essentials but with the architecture and decor of France's Second Empire.

Lenox Hotel
MAP L5 ▪ 61 Exeter St, 02116 ▪ 617 536 5300 ▪ www.lenoxhotel.com ▪ $$$
Known for its exemplary service, luxurious and modern comfort, historic elegance, and eco-innovation, this Back Bay boutique hotel near Copley Square has served Boston visitors since 1900. Several of the spacious corner rooms have wood-burning fireplaces. Dine at the City Table on New England seasonal fare, or at the Sólás authentic Irish Pub.

Sonder 907 Main
MAP S3 ▪ 907 Main St, Cambridge, MA 02114 ▪ 617 300 0956 ▪ www. 907main.com ▪ $$$
Shoehorned between the MIT campus and the dining and music scene of Central Square, this boutique lodging has an urban loft feel with its industrial elements and exposed brick. Wi-Fi is included in the price of the room.

Mid-Range Hotels

Cambria Hotel Boston
MAP D2 ▪ 86 W Broadway, South Boston, 02127 ▪ 617 752 6681 ▪ www.choicehotels.com ▪ $$
The Cambria might be a little further away for those wanting to focus on Boston's main attractions, but it is conveniently located beside the Red Line's Broadway stop in Southie. Expect soothing rooms, with a gray and white colour scheme, complete with a good work desk and reliable Wi-Fi.

The Charlesmark
MAP L5 ▪ 655 Boylston St, 02116 ▪ 617 247 1212 ▪ www.charlesmarkhotel. com ▪ $$
Set in a historical 1892 Back Bay townhouse, this boutique hotel has compact but ergonomic rooms that feature custom-made furniture, light-toned woodwork, and smart Italian tilework. Breakfast is included in the astonishingly low (for the area) rates.

Courtyard Boston Downtown
MAP N5 ▪ 275 Tremont St, 02116 ▪ 617 426 1400 ▪ www.marriott. com ▪ $$
Located at the edge of the city's Theater District, this 1920s tower hotel underwent restoration to give fresh glitter to its dramatic public spaces. The stylish hotel features crystal chandeliers, marble columns, and small rooms with first-rate amenities.

Fairfield Inn & Suites Boston Cambridge
MAP F2 ▪ 215 Monsignor O'Brien Hway, Cambridge, 02141 ▪ 617 621 1999 ▪ www.fairfieldboston cambridge.com ▪ $$
This contemporary hotel is set across the Charles River from Downtown. Rooms here feature an ergonomic workstation. There's free Wi-Fi, free hot breakfast, and access to a 24-hour fitness center.

Harborside Inn
MAP Q3 ▪ 185 State St, 02109 ▪ 617 723 7500 ▪ www.harborsideinn boston.com ▪ $$
A modest boutique hotel, Harborside is set in a historic 1858 spice warehouse. Rooms have wood floors, exposed brick walls, oriental rugs, and traditional furnishings.

Hyatt Centric
MAP Q4 ▪ 54–68 Devonshire St, 02109 ▪ 617 720 1234 ▪ www. hyatt.com ▪ $$
Sleek and modern, Hyatt Centric is located within walking distance of historic landmarks and iconic sights. Sweeping views of the city can be enjoyed from rooms on higher floors. The pricing is higher during the week than on the weekends. Amenities such as a 24-hour fitness center, pet-friendly rooms, and comple-mentary Wi-Fi will add to your experience.

Inn at St Botolph
MAP E5 ▪ 99 St Botolph St, 02116 ▪ 617 236 8099 ▪ www.innatstbotolph.com ▪ $$
This redbrick townhouse boutique hotel is perfect for a romantic getaway. The sunny rooms have a contemporary design and queen-size beds. Aiming for an individualized experience, the hotel provides private keyless entry. The staff here is very attentive.

Kendall Hotel
MAP E3 ▪ 350 Main St, Cambridge, 02142 ▪ 617 577 1300 ▪ www.kendallhotel.com ▪ $$
An artist-architect couple transformed this century-old Cambridge firehouse into a boutique hotel. The 77 rooms are decorated with an Americana folk art theme. Don't miss the Rooftop Retreat.

Sheraton Commander
MAP B1 ▪ 16 Garden St, Cambridge, 02138 ▪ 617 547 4800 ▪ www.sheratoncommander.com ▪ $$
Harvard Square's original hotel, built in 1927, has elegant contemporary decor. Some rooms are small, but public areas are pleasant and lively, and the Cambridge Common location is enchanting.

Staypineapple, Boston
MAP M6 ▪ 26 Chandler St, 02116 ▪ 866 866 7977 ▪ www.staypineapple.com ▪ $$
A classic brick townhouse inn located in South End, this hotel is just a few steps away from the city's historical sites and great stores and restaurants.

It provides luxurious bedding and high-speed Wi-Fi in space-efficient modern rooms.

Westin Boston Waterfront
MAP P4 ▪ 425 Summer St, 02210 ▪ 617 532 4600 ▪ www.starwoodhotels.com ▪ $$
Connected to the Boston Convention and Exhibition Center, this huge property serves business travelers well. Rooms offer great city views.

B&Bs

Bowers House
9 Bowers Ave, Somerville, 02144 ▪ 617 680 6828 ▪ www.bowershousebnb.com ▪ $
The rooms in this friendly B&B are modern and individually decorated. The house is located in the hip Davis Square and is just a short subway ride away from all the main sights in the city.

A Friendly Inn at Harvard
MAP C1 ▪ 1673 Cambridge St, 02138 ▪ 617 547 7851 ▪ www.afinow.com ▪ $
This Queen Anne-style house is just steps from Harvard Square and the museums. The great location, gracious hospitality, and all mod cons, including internet access, make this a very popular hotel, particularly with visiting scholars and prospective students.

Oasis Guest House
22 Edgerly Rd, 02115 ▪ 617 267 2262 ▪ www.oasisgh.com ▪ $
Close to Berklee School of Music, the Hynes Convention Center, and

Symphony Hall, Oasis offers rooms in a townhouse located on a quiet one-way street a little removed from the hub-bub of Massachusetts Avenue. Guests can make use of a small, shared outdoor deck.

Clarendon Square Inn
MAP F6 ▪ 198 W Brookline St, 02118 ▪ 617 536 2229 ▪ www.clarendonsquare.com ▪ $$
Comfortable, spacious, and sophisticated guest rooms and luxury suites are housed in a six-story South End Boston townhouse built in 1860. They offer designer fabrics, private bathrooms in limestone and marble, and the latest technology. There is no elevator.

Irving House
MAP C1 ▪ 24 Irving St, Cambridge, 02138 ▪ 617 547 4600 ▪ www.irvinghouse.com ▪ $$
Visiting scholars favor this welcoming B&B, which is set in a leafy neighborhood near Harvard University. The rooms range from small singles to spacious doubles – a few rooms have shared bathrooms. Breakfast is included in the price.

Newbury Guest House
MAP K5 ▪ 261 Newbury St, 02116 ▪ 617 670 6000 ▪ www.newburyguesthouse.com ▪ $$
Several Back Bay homes have been linked to create this 32-room guesthouse. Rooms vary in size, but tend to be cozy with eclectic furnishings. Good value for the location.

Budget Hotels, Inns, and Hostels

Hostelling International

MAP P5 ■ 19 Stuart St, 02116 ■ 617 536 9455 ■ www.bostonhostel.org ■ $

Located downtown, just a short walk from popular sights, this modern hostel offers single-sex dorms with bunk beds, or private en-suite rooms with TVs. Continental breakfast is included, and a communal kitchen and laundry rooms are available.

Hotel 1868

MAP J5 ■ 1868 Massachusetts Ave, Cambridge 02140 ■ 617 499 2998 ■ www. hotel1868.com ■ $

This stylish hotel is just across the street from the Porter Square "T" and commuter rail station. It features an on-site gym and a café.

The Revolution Hotel

MAP M6 ■ 40 Berkeley St, 02116 ■ 617 848 9200 ■ www.therevolution hotel.com ■ $

Chic and fun, this brightly tiled South End inn enjoys a truly hip aesthetic. The rooms are small but designed with modern comforts in mind. Some rooms have shared bathrooms down the hall.

Constitution Inn

MAP G2 ■ 150 3rd Ave, Charlestown Navy Yard, Charlestown, 02129 ■ 617 241 8400 ■ www. constitutioninn.org ■ $$

A 147-room facility in Charlestown Navy Yard, the Constitution Inn serves military personnel, but welcomes all. Rooms are clean and modern, and guests can use the fitness center with pool and sauna free of charge.

DoubleTree

Columbia Point, Dorchester ■ 240 Mt Vernon St, 02125 ■ 617 822 3600 ■ www.double tree3.hilton.com ■ $$

This hotel is located near the HarborWalk and the John F. Kennedy Library and Museum. There's a free shuttle to the airport and local restaurants.

Freepoint Hotel

220 Alewife Brook Pkwy, Cambridge, 02138 ■ 617 491 8000 ■ www.free pointhotel.com ■ $$

Situated near the Alewife "T" station on the edge of Cambridge, Freepoint boasts chic style that suggests luxury, at a reasonable price.

Hampton Inn

191 Monsignor O'Brien Hwy, Cambridge, 02141 ■ 617 494 5300 ■ www. hamptoninn3.hilton.com ■ $$

This chain hotel features high-speed internet in all rooms as well as free underground parking. Rooms are modest but include a good-sized desk area, making it popular with business travelers on a limited budget.

Holiday Inn Express

MAP F2 ■ 250 Monsignor O'Brien Hwy, Cambridge, 02141 ■ 617 577 7600 ■ www.hiecambridge. com ■ $$

All of the rooms in this roadside motel have good work areas, microwaves, and refrigerators. There's limited free parking and it's only a short walk to the Lechmere "T" stop.

Inn at Longwood Medical Center

342 Longwood Ave, 02115 ■ 617 731 4700 ■ www. innatlongwood.com ■ $$

Attractive and comfortable, this is a 144-room inn set in the Longwood Medical Area. Families of patients get the best rates but it is open to all travelers.

La Quinta Inn and Suites

23 Cummings St, Somerville, 02145 ■ 617 625 5300 ■ www.lq.com ■ $$

Just a short walk from the MBTA Orange Line, this inn offers an airport shuttle service. Spacious rooms and suites have tasteful decor, cable TV, as well as internet.

Porter Square Hotel

1924 Massachusetts Ave, 02140 ■ 617 499 3399 ■ www.theportersquare hotel.com ■ $$

Across the street from Lesley University and a subway stop beyond Harvard, this handsome hotel features an excellent desk area – even in the "petite" rooms. The hotel has a French-style bistro.

Yotel

65 Seaport Ave, 02210 ■ 617 377 4747 ■ www. yotel.com ■ $$

Technologically driven, and ergonomically designed, Yotel maximizes comfort and aesthetic. The rooms are space-efficient, decorated in cool tones. The list of amenities go beyond the usual, including a concierge app and a resident robot.

For a key to hotel price categories see p146

General Index

Acknowledgments

Author

Patricia Harris and David Lyon write about travel, food, fine arts, and popular culture for many publications including *Boston Magazine*, *Boston Globe*, *Yankee*, *Robb Report*, and hungrytravelers. com. They also co-wrote the Dorling Kindersley *Eyewitness Travel Guide to Boston*.

Jonathan Schultz is a travel writer based in Portland, Maine. He has contributed extensive local content to *Boston Magazine*, Boston.citysearch.com; LosAngeles.citysearch.com; as well as having compiled a guide to Boston for Z Publishing.

Additional contributors
Paul Franklin, Nancy Mikula

Publishing Director Georgina Dee

Publisher Vivien Antwi

Design Director Phil Ormerod

Editorial Michelle Crane, Rebecca Flynn, Rachel Fox, Fay Franklin, Hayley Maher, Freddie Marriage, Fíodhna Ní Ghríofa, Scarlett O'Hara, Sally Schafer, Ankita Sharma, Neil Simpson

Cover Design Maxine Pedliham, Vinita Venugopal

Design Marisa Renzullo

Picture Research Susie Peachey, Ellen Root, Lucy Sienkowska, Oran Tarjan

Cartography Subhashree Bharti, Suresh Kumar, James Macdonald, Simonetta Giori, Dominic Beddow

Senior Production Editor Jason Little

Production Linda Dare

Factchecker Pat Harris & David Lyon

Proofreader Kathryn Glendenning

Indexer Hilary Bird

Illustrator Lee Redmond

First edition created by Departure Lounge, London

Revisions Sophie Adam, Parnika Bagla, Marta Bescos, Subhashree Bharti, Dipika Dasgupta, Marc Di Duca, Alice Fewery, Rebecca Flynn, Nayan Keshan, Sumita Khatwani, Shikha Kulkarni, Suresh Kumar, Maresa Manara, Alison McGill, Bhavika Mathur, Chhavi Nagpal, George Nimmo, Rebecca Parton, Bandana Puri, Vagisha Pushp, Azeem Siddiqui, Beverly Smart, Priyanka Thakur, Rachel Thompson, Stuti Tiwari, Ankita Awasthi Tröger, Åsa Westerlund Tanveer Zaidi

Commissioned Photography John Coletti, Demetrio Carrasco, Rough Guides/Angus Osborn, Rough Guides/Susannah Sayler, Tony Souter, Linda Whitwam.

Picture Credits

The publisher would like to thank the following for their kind permission to reproduce these photographs:
Key: a-above; b-below/bottom; c-centre; f-far; l-left; r-right; t-top

Alamy Images: Hank Abernathy 101tl; Marcus Baker 72tl; Alastair Balderstone 75cla; M. Scott Brauer 74crb; Darryl Brooks 92b; David Coleman 133clb; Stephen Coyne 7tr; Shay Culligan 106cl; Ian Dagnall 56br; Ian G Dagnall 57tl, 95tr; Randy Duchaine 51cr; Michael Dwyer 38cra; Eagle Visions Photography / Craig Lovell 122tr; Raymond Forbes 103cla; Jeff Greenberg 6 of 6/ *The Thinker, Frogs of Tadpole Playground* (2003) by David Phillips The City of Boston, The Boston Art Commission 53cr; Della Huff 4cra, 4crb, 98ca; Andre Jenny 37tl; JLImages 18bc; Kim Karpeles 53tr; LOOK/Elan Fleisher 83tl, 99cl; Mary Evans Picture Library 42tl; Terry Mathews 25crb; Paul Matzner 116cra; Megapress 52br; Debra Millet 104tl; Steven Milne 13crb; MJ Photography 85cr; NATUREWOLRD 47cla; B. O'Kane 23b; Michael Neelon 18-19ca; Niday Picture Library /*Portrait of Samuel Adams* (1772) by John Singleton Copley 44clb; Nikreates 24cla, 42cb; Sean Pavon 1; Stuart Pearce 11cr, 98bl; North Wind Picture Archives 43tr; Anthony Pleva 130c; Prisma Bildagentur AG/Heeb Christian 11tl; Valery Rizzo 61tl; Rosalrene Betancourt 7 18cla; Science History Images 14t; Lee Snider 80cla; Kumar Sriskandan 67bl; Superstock/George Ostertag 36–7.

Aquitaine: 113tr.

Banks Fish House: Allison Cullen 65br; **Barbara Lynch Gruppo:** 63tl, 69tl, 111br. **Beacon Hill Chocolates:** 84cb. **Berklee College of Music:** 55tr. **Bostonian Society:** 12ca. **Boston Playwrights Theatre:** Kalman Zabarsky 118cl. **Boston Symphony Orchestra:** Marco Borggreve 54t; Stu Rosner 117tr. **Courtesy of the Museum of Science, Boston:** Michael Malyszko 16cra, 17tr. **Museum of Fine Arts, Boston:** 11cra, 28c, 28cb, 29tl, 29crb, 30ca, 30bl, 31tl, 31cr; *Mr and Mrs Isaac Winsow* (1773) by John Singleton Copley 28br; *Lullaby: Madame Augustine Roulin Rocking a Cradle (La Berceuse)* (1889) by Vincent van Gogh 31bl. **Bridgeman Images:** AA World Travel Library 33tr; Houston 45tr.

Multicultural Arts Centre: Yi-Lin Hung Photography 124clb. **Children's Museum, Boston:** Paul Specht 52tl, 96tl. **Club Cafe:** 58tl. **Corbis:** Bettmann 22tl; Massimo Borchi 2tl, 8–9; National Geographic Creative/Brian J. Skerry 52b; Richard T. Nowitz 10cra; and Andria Patino/ *Boston Women Memorial* (2003) by Meredith Gang Bergman The City of Boston, The Boston Art Commission 88–9.

Courtesy of the artist and Barbara Krakow Gallery: work by Jackie Ferrara at "Surface: Summer Group Show", June 8, 2013 – July 26, 2013. 90bl.

Courtesy of the Nichols House Museum, Boston, MA: Gilded bronze bust of wreathed Victory (1902) by Augustus Saint-Gaudens 80tr.

David Lyon & Patricia Harris: 84tl, 90c, 104br, 110tr, 111c, 120tr, 126c, 126bl, 134b.

Dreamstime.com: Americanspirit 95bl; Anastassiyal 127tl; Berniephillips 11br; Jon Bilous 12br, 46bl, 81t, 96b; Joaquin Ossorio Castillo 77cla; Angel Claudio 49t; Jerry Coli 16crb; David931 19bl; Dejavu Designs 48br; Demerzel21 100cla; Songquan Deng 86tl; Kristy Durbridge 36bc, 52tl; Joachim Eckel 22cb; Elena Elisseeva 3tl, 78–9; F11photo 13c, 47tr, 102t, 107t; Ritu Jethani 102cb, 131br; Wangkun Jia 94tr; Mary Lane 101br; Chee-onn Leong 4b, 11clb, 32bl, 76t;